THE HIDDEN SECRET OF GOD: THE BIBLE DECODED BY NEVILLE GODDARD

VOLUME ONE

ALIO PUBLISHING GROUP

Copyright © 2023 by ALIO Publishing Group

All rights reserved.

No portion of this book may be reproduced in any form without express written permission from the publisher, except as permitted by U.S. copyright law.

Contents

Introduction	1
1. Many Mansions	3
2. The Law	24
3. The Hidden Secret of God	32
4. Grace vs Law	46
5. Seedtime and Harvest	59
6. The True Apostle Paul	73
7. The Identical Harvest	89
Glossary of Cited Verses	105
About the Author	107
Also By ALIO Publishing Group	108

INTRODUCTION

*"The truth – if it truly is true – will not run in fright
from the slightest sight of questions
offered by those earnestly seeking to confirm what is true."*

As of this writing, it is the year 2023, and the Holy Bible remains after centuries one of the most hotly-debated texts. Every aspect of its existence, from the authentic author (or authors) of it, to the meaning of its many messages, continue to act as a catalyst of controversy and contention among people across faiths and locations.

Why hasn't a book that holds such weight and significance for mankind been definitively explained and made plain for the benefit of all? Why is it that a book containing the guidance and instructions from our very creator (to those that believe) has been more often employed in the oppressing of populations, rather than liberating them? It isn't an accident that the so-called most intelligent life-form on Earth struggles the most with just existing.

It doesn't have to be that way. Instead of causing further division, the Bible's words - when fully understood - can connect people. Confusion and doubt have no place in a room occupied by the truth. In *The Hidden Secret of God*, a series of lectures given in the mid-20th century by the late Neville Goddard (recognized today as one of the pioneers of the law of assumption concept) will clarify the deeper intent and meaning behind many biblical verses.

In doing so, lines will be drawn between the literal and the figurative; the physical, and the metaphysical; the allegory, and the actual. As its editor, it is my earnest wish that by the end of this book, you will not only feel closer to the Creator, but to creation as well.

And just to be perfectly clear: one does not have to consider themselves a Christian to be here. As long as life has existed, there has been that which is true. Truth predates religion, if we're being honest.

To gain the most from this material, it is advised to approach it with the brilliant simplicity of a child. Children are generally explorative and inquisitive, which affords them a certain natural measure of genius that often dwindles as we progress into adulthood (an unfortunate side effect of the incessant reinforcement of contradictory indoctrination typically embedded in us without repose).

As you progress through this collection of what may seem to be unorthodox teachings, take care to do so with an open mind that is able to apply practical critical thinking, and willing to challenge mental comfort zones.

The truth is frequently far more simple than we expect. Receive these words openly, but do not be reluctant to put them through the paces, and under fire. Information gained ought to always be tested for its value. What remains is what you trust; what stays is what you retain.

The Hidden Secret of God reveals truths that are not held back by some malevolent entity or organization of ill-intent. Rather, it details truths that have been "hidden" in plain sight, due to man's collective tendency to overlook the obvious...most often as a by-product of blindly adopting untested information from others. I myself have faith in your power as a being bestowed with a conscious, reasoning mind to determine the potential validity of what's offered here, put it through your own critical processes, test, weigh, and finally: discern appropriately.

In the words of the late Dr. Blair: *"There is no truth, until **you** decide what truth is."*

One

Many Mansions

"Our Father's house has many mansions." You may be familiar with the subject from the 14th chapter of the book of John: "Let not your hearts be troubled: ye believe in God, believe also in me. In my Father's house are many mansions. Were it not so, would I have told you that I am going to prepare a place for you? And when I go, I will come again and receive you to myself, that where I am, there you may be also." (John 14:1-3, Moffatt's translation) Now, who is this one speaking? Scripture tells us it is Jesus Christ. The chapter affirms it.

Arthur Chamber said: *"It takes a great imagination to follow Jesus Christ, and I, for one, have been lacking in such imagination."* At least, he was big enough to confess it. I have met many, when you begin to discuss Scripture with them, who will always ask one simple question: "Have you read the New Testament in Greek?" Well, my confession is always: "No, I do not, and cannot, read Greek." Then, of course, they have that supercilious attitude: "Well, then you haven't read it in Greek! Isn't that strange?"

This happened just about three months ago, and I said that is one of the questions that Aldous Huxley asked me. He read it in Greek. I said to him what I said to this gentleman who asked me: "Isn't it peculiar? Aldous read it in Greek from the original. You read it in Greek in the original." (In this century he is really tops. He is gone from this world now.) I said to him: "You know, Aldous, you read it in Greek and you read it in English, and yet you don't understand it."

So, you ask me: have I read it in Greek? No, I can't read it in Greek, but I've read it in English, and I understand it - understand it because I've experienced it, and you haven't. Well, the last time that question was asked me was three months ago. He was perfectly still after I said to him: "You don't understand it." So, what did his Greek do? So tonight, we will go into this great mystery - for it is a mystery.

Paul uses the word "mystery" concerning this story of Christ no less than twenty-odd times. He said: "Great is the mystery . . ." All through his letters he is speaking of the mystery. It is not history, for history is not a mystery; it is simply a record of the facts. Well, this is not a record of the facts of a secular nature, for the Bible is not secular history. It's salvation history. So here, what are these "mansions" spoken of? They are states. All states are eternal, and they exist now. All states exist in the human imagination, and the human imagination is the Lord Jesus Christ. That's God. There is no other God. And all things exist in him now!

We have to make the adjustment: think of an infinite number of states - anything you can think of - it exists now. Man passes through states, like a traveler who passes through places, through cities. Well, the man who is passing through a state, like the traveler who is passing through a place, may suppose that the place that he has passed through exists no more, as a man passing through a state thinks the state through which he has passed exists no more.

Wouldn't it be silly when I leave this city to feel that because I have departed, that the city has ceased to exist? They remain for anyone to enter, and when they are in it, it seems to be the only reality and everything else in the world seems a mere shadow. When you enter into a city or a state, that state seems to be the only substance. Every state in the world exists now.

Now, the first creative act recorded in Scripture is in the second verse of the 1st chapter of Genesis: "...and the Spirit of God moved..." Whatever takes place is that movement within God. And God is our own wonderful, human imagination. So whatever takes place is simply movement within God. How does He now move? That's the secret: how to go into these states and make them real, make them alive in our world. It's a very simple process - very simple - but you and I have to act to do it. It won't do it itself; we have to do it.

When we move into the state and clothe ourselves with the state, the state then takes on an external tone and becomes objective to our sight, as this room is now objective because we're in it. All these states are just as real as this room once we occupy them. So, "in my Father's house are many mansions," numberless mansions. "Were it not so, would I have told you that I go to prepare a place for you? And when I go...I will come again and receive you to myself, that where I am, there ye shall be also." (John 14: 2, 3)

As I stand here, my adjustment is only in my imagination. I don't walk into the place - I don't travel into it. I simply adjust it here: close my eyes to the obvious, and then assume that it is here and clothe myself with the reality of the state of my selection. Now, I open my eyes upon this room and this room denies the reality of what I've done in my imagination.

But wait - just wait! I can't forget it and I can't rub it out. It will take the place of this. But why don't I remember it? Every natural effect in this world has a spiritual cause, and not a natural. A natural cause only seems; it is a delusion of the perishing vegetable memory. Man's memory fades, and when he's confronted with his own harvest he doesn't recognize his harvest.

He denies that at any moment in time did he entertain vividly, with emotion, such things that are happening in his world, because his memory fades and he doesn't remember. So, he questions the law (if he ever heard of it). He questions: "How could this thing happen to me?" (Haven't you heard that time and again?) Or have your heard the statement: "Why should it happen to him? He is so nice. He is an altogether wonderful chap. Why should it happen to him?"

Here's a question, just before I left L.A. "Why should these things happen to Dad and to Mother? Certainly you know, above all people, they don't deserve it." It's not a matter of deserving. These are states. At one moment in time they entertained this with feeling, with intense feeling, and then these things happen. And they might have passed judgment on one who had a similar condition, and relate the condition to some unlovely thing they know of that person and think God was getting even. Yet, they are ardent churchgoers, members of the church.

One is on the altar guild; the other is a trustee of the church. He's a banker by profession. They really devote themselves to the service of the church. Well, what has that to do with one entertaining these emotions with feeling, intense feeling, and then forgetting it, not knowing that the effect (when it takes place - and it is a natural and a real effect) that it is related to a spiritual cause, and the spiritual cause is nothing more than a motion within themselves.

Within themselves they move, and having moved, they are going to project that state into which they fell, either wisely or unwisely. And when it comes into the world for recognition they don't recognize their own harvest. But there is no other way that it could come into the world.

So, "The Spirit of God moved..." and then the whole vast world began to appear. He moved. Now, motion can be detected only by a change of position relative to another object. If this very moment we were hurtled into space, all in the same motion, I wouldn't know, and you wouldn't know, that we were moving. I can only detect motion if I can observe a motion relative to an object that seems to be stationary relative to me. And so, I must have a frame of reference against which I move.

So, the frame of reference: I stand here - I have a frame of reference. I have friends who know (or think they know) where I stand in the world. They think they know what I stand for, how I live, and that's what they believe. Well, in my mind's eye I see that frame of reference, and then I let them see me differently. I didn't go any place - I allowed them to see me differently. Well, if they see me differently then I must have moved. So in my mind's eye I construct a scene implying the fulfillment of my dream, and then as I see it, I accept it as true and believe that they accept it as true of me. So I change it.

If I change it within myself and use that frame of reference, and the same reveals a change in me, well then, I have moved. That is the secret of all creation in the world: "And the Spirit of God moved." And the minute He moved, things appeared. "Let there be light."

Let everything now that this is implying appear in my world, for the potency is in its implication. Well, what does it imply - this motion? Well, it implies that they now see in me what I would like them to see. As they see me in that light, I am actually saying (without the use of words): "Let there be light on it now. Let it come into the world that the whole world may see it." See what?

See the motion that I produced within myself. For when we are told: "The Spirit of God moved," that's no more than your own wonderful human imagination moving relative to a frame of reference, and so you move. How is this taught in Scripture? It's taught in the most beautiful manner. It's told as a story. These are not secular stories; these are profound truths.

Now, Rebecca conceives; she's pregnant. Isaac prays that his wife will be given a child - given a son - and the Lord responded, as we are told, and she conceived. Well, then there was trouble within her womb, and she wondered: "Why should these things be? If this is so, why should I live?", for, there was a conflict within herself. And the Lord said to her: "Two nations are within your womb, and two manners of people, born of you, shall be divided; one shall be stronger than the other, and the elder shall serve the younger." (This is told us in the 25th chapter of the book of Genesis.)

Now, as the story unfolds, the one comes out second, and he has no hair. His name is Jacob, which means a "supplanter." He supplants, he takes the place of the other. The one that came out first was covered with hair all over. He is called Esau. Jacob supplants him by deception. He deceives his father into believing that he was his son, Esau. How did he do it? He clothed himself with hair and came to his father, and the father said: "Your voice is the voice of Jacob. Come close, come near, that I may feel," for the father was blind. Isaac was blind, and he could not see.

So he came near, and as he came near and the father felt him, he said: "The voice is the voice of Jacob, but the hands are the hands of Esau," and he blessed him. And when he blessed him he gave him the birthright that belonged to the first son. When the first son came in from the hunt, bringing what the father had requested (venison) he said: "Who are you?" He said: "I am your son, Esau." "Well," he said, "I have just blessed my son Esau." He said: "That was Jacob," the deceiver. (This is the second time he has deceived him.)

Then the father said, "I have blessed him, and I cannot take back the blessing. You have to serve him." Well now, tell that story and what does it mean? Here is my Esau. You are my Esau. This room is Esau. This is stronger than my subjective state. How stronger? This to me is the utmost: I am here, and everything in my world that I can touch and see now and sense. This is the strong, strong son - my surface. The subjective state is what? I can paint a word picture of it, but that's not real. But I'm going to make it real.

So I shut my eyes, and - closing my eyes to the facts of life, to the obvious things - I am blind. So, Isaac was blind. I close my eyes; I don't see it. Then I persuade myself that I am what I would like to be, instead of what reason dictates and my senses dictate. Well, in that projected state, I clothe myself with the other, although I can't accept it right now. Imagination is spiritual sensation. Now, take an object. I will just lead you in words. Take a tennis ball in your imaginary hands and feel it. You can feel it.

To show you the difference, take a baseball. Can you discriminate between the two? Well now, take a ping-pong ball. Can you discriminate between the three? If these are non-existent, you couldn't discriminate. How can you say that these do not exist and say that you can tell the difference between non-existent things? They do not, at the moment, exist in your outer mind's senses - they don't. But they exist! All things exist now in the human imagination. That's where you felt it; you felt it in your imagination, and imagination is spiritual sensation. Well then, what does that mean? "

I saw it in my mind's eye, and I felt the three different kinds of balls." Well, what does it mean? Well, now to test one. Take this and apply it to anything in the world. Apply it to mountains; apply it to anything, and if you accept what you've done to test it in your imagination, just wait. "The vision has its own appointed hour, it ripens, it will flower; if it be long, then wait, for it is sure, and it will not be late." (Habakkuk 2:3, Moffatt's translation) It will come on time!

Let me share with you an experience of just a few months ago of this friend of mine - a very marvelous chap - an executive in a very prominent advertising agency in Los Angeles (he comes to all the meetings). Here are two short ones: He said, "I was driving home, and then it dawned upon me: You know that April 15th is just around the corner, and you could do with some cash for Uncle Sam." Now, he receives a very large salary, but he spends it and he lives a lovely, generous life.

He has a lovely home and three children. He maintains a beautiful home, but he never thought in terms of these moments in time when we are confronted with Uncle Sam's outstretched hand and he wants a part of what you earn. Well, you can't say "No" to him; you've got to pay him. So here comes around the corner the 15th of April, and he could use some cash. "Riding home," he said, "this is what I did. I simply imagined, and I made a game of it.

I imagined that it was raining gently, but the rain was little green pieces of paper. It was money coming gently upon me, and I could feel it - actually feel the gentle rain of paper money dropping upon me, and I had stopped. I had done this for about two or three minutes, and then the traffic demanded all of my attention; and so I broke it. When I went home that night I thought it was great fun and I'd try it again. I could feel it actually descending upon me like a gentle rain.

The next day was the 14th of April, and sitting at my desk (not paying any attention to it, really) the boss comes in, and he said to me: 'You have a 10% raise, and it's retroactive as of the first of the month', and gave me a check for a 10% raise." And he makes a *very* big salary. So, 10% of a very large salary, and it was retroactive to the first of the month - here, within a matter of moments, his feeling was granted as an actual fact! He didn't have it before he started, and now he has it. The vision came to flower at the appointed hour. He needed it on the 15th; and here, just before the 15th, a man comes through with a check and tells him that it is retroactive to the first, at 10% beyond what he got last month.

Now, this is a story that I have at home, at the hotel, in his own hand. He didn't confine me to some secrecy. He told it to me - not in confidence, but that I may share it with others to encourage them to try it. "Now," he said, "I went home a couple of months before, and my wife began to tell me a very unlovely story - unlovely in the sense that we love the little girl. She's 14 months old, and we know her grandmother well.

Of course we know the mother, but we are closer to the grandmother, and the grandmother told my wife that the little girl began to develop bumps in her neck - little swellings. So they took her to the hospital for observation. They made a biopsy and 5 doctors brought in the negative verdict that it was malignant; it was cancer."

Well, in a child of 14 months that is fatal, because you are developing. You can arrest cancer if you are my age because you are not building any more - and they drop from this world by some other means - because at my age if I was told I had cancer, it doesn't mean that that will be the cause of my future departure from this world. For I am not building any longer; I am just holding my own. Well, a little child of 14 months builds rapidly, so whatever is in her is building rapidly. With cancer, in no time they are gone. So the grandmother was scared; the mother was scared.

But as his wife was telling my friend, he said: "I allowed her voice to tell me completely different. I heard just enough. She kept on talking, but she didn't know from my expression that I wasn't listening. I didn't hear one word after I heard what she said, and as she kept on building the picture, her voice faded from me. And then I reconstructed what she said, and I had her tell me that the whole thing was false. Although there were 5 doctors, each agreeing that this thing was malignant and therefore fatal, I let it fade completely and brought in a complete reversal of that verdict."

Now the grandmother asked that they keep the child a little longer at the hospital that they could still bring in another. So, they made another biopsy from a different section of the neck. A 6th doctor was brought in. "I am sorry to disagree with my men in the profession, but it is not malignant and it is not cancer." They then were called in to make a third, and they confessed that they were wrong because she couldn't possibly have had cancer and today not have cancer. So they had to justify it.

They could not for one moment; they confessed they were wrong. He said: "That's all right with me. The child now lives and she has no cancer. Why should I go out and tell them: No, they were right in the first time, but prayer to the only God that exists can make all things possible? With God, all things are possible, but you don't know who God is, so you believe in your technique. It's perfectly all right."

He said: "Now, my wife told me exactly what I knew." The grandmother is now telling it all over the neighborhood, and now they look upon me as a miracle man - which is unfortunate, because it will make life difficult for me in the neighborhood." He said: "I'm no miracle man; I simply learned through you who God is. And if all things are possible to God, and God is my own imagination, can't I imagine what I want to imagine and persuade myself of the reality of the state imagined? Well, I did, and the child now is free of what they called cancer. But to justify their own decision and not say: 'Well, we were wrong', they now say it could not have been cancer or therefore she could not have overcome it."

So, here is that story I've just told you, plus the raise in salary, and unnumbered things the man lives by. He is not interested in the Promise. Well that's all right. He's a businessman, and he has to pay rent, buy clothes for his children and his wife and himself. And he's more interested in the Law, and so he's always writing these stories concerning the Law. If perchance I get off and week after week, I'm stressing the Promise, I can see Dick - that night he isn't going to come. Well, it doesn't interest him but it's perfectly all right, because we're living in the world of Caesar, and we've got to master this Law and not pass the buck and blame others for the things that are happening in our world, for in my Father's house are unnumbered mansions.

It sets me now on my feet to become discriminating, to become selective. Into what mansion will I go this night? Into what state of consciousness will I go this night? For, if I occupy it, even though I forget it tomorrow, it will not be forgotten. I have planted the seed, and in time - and on time - it will come up as a harvest. Whether I recognize my own planting or not, it's coming into my world. So, why not devote some time every day to planting lovely things in this world?

People will say: "Well, all right - thorns are real, aren't they?" Oh, yes, thorns are real, but aren't roses real too? Do you want to go out and really pluck thorns - or roses? If I am going to dwell on the thorns, well, I will trade it and leave it for a flower for the Son of Man. Why can't I think in terms of roses? I'm not denying that thorns are real. The things you see in the headlines, all these things - "Nixon declares war," or something, why couldn't they've told that same story differently, for in man's mind the word war has a certain association? Big headlines: "Nixon Declares War" on something.

Another paper more modestly tells it, and they will say: "Nixon Takes Issue" with this, that, and the other. But no, we have to simply frighten the reader to make him buy the paper. If he's declared war, you will read the second line in smaller print, because you might think he's declared war on Russia. So, the big headline, and then you read what he is really concerned about - some little issue. So here in my Father's house are these unnumbered mansions, numberless states of consciousness.

Learn to discriminate between the man and his present state, so that you meet someone and he's a wonderful being, and in your eyes he seems so just and so honest. Another one is despicable. But when you know they are only states, you will actually see that you *"do not consider either the just or the wicked to be the supreme state, but to be, every one of them, states of the sleep which the soul may fall into in its deadly dreams of good and evil."* (William Blake, from "The Last Judgment")

So the one who is now so just - he may not be conscious of the fact that he has moved into that state literally, and therefore really is a just man, for he is only expressing the state in which he has placed himself. He might have been placed in that state deliberately, or accidentally. If it is done deliberately - good! Then he'll know how to get out of it and to continue in all the lovely states in this world. But if he fell into it, appearing as a just man, he could easily fall out of it, and then tomorrow you will read in the paper where he is not so just after all.

So when I know that these are only states...you don't save men, for in every man there is God, and God-in-man is man's own wonderful, human imagination. But if he doesn't know that he will say, as most people say, "Oh, it's just my imagination. It means nothing. It means absolutely nothing. I can imagine whatever I want because I didn't do it," - he doesn't know he's going to do it. You dwell upon a thing for a long while and make it real, so you're always coming back to it. That state to which I most often return constitutes my dwelling place.

You'll find a certain person - after a little while, he's always talking on a certain subject, and he's coming back to it and back to it and back to it. He may be talking about poverty, and always talking poverty. Well then, follow him. He moves his home, he moves his job - he moves everything, because the state to which I most constantly return constitutes the place where I dwell. So follow my imagination. Where does it dwell most often in the course of a day? That's my dwelling place.

Well, you can start now, and for twenty-four hours dwell in security - not security from the government, because...no, you have it, you've earned it, either through your talent or in some normal but dignified manner. You didn't steal it; you have it in a marvelous way. Well then, you dwell upon that state and feel what it would be like if it were true. For you see: when the man was blind, he emphasized the one thing, which seemed to be the easiest of all senses actually to apply: that's feeling. He said: "Come close, my son, that I may feel you." He couldn't see him; he was blind.

He did use another sense, called "smell." He said: "You smell and you feel like my son Esau." Esau had hair all over him. Well, isn't that the most external thing in the world? The first thing you encounter of a man is hair. You may not even see it, but under the microscope we are all, like a monkey, completely covered with hair. Now, the other one had no hair. He's left completely subjective. So one comes out into the world covered with hair, and you have a lengthy image of a boy with hair all over. It hasn't a thing to do with a little child who came into this world covered with hair!

It means the external world, for that is the most external thing in the world. When you read that John the Baptist came and he had a girdle made of leather and he wore a shirt of hair, it isn't a man with a girdle of leather and a camel's hair coat. That tells you that his story is external. All that he has to say is completely external: "Thou shalt not." In other words, he came neither to eat nor drink, and his whole world was one of bias against his own appetites.

So he felt that by doing violence to himself he could gain the Kingdom of Heaven. Then we are told by the one who had no hair: "Christ in you is subjective," and he said: "John the Baptist and all those born of women, none is greater than John the Baptist: nevertheless, I say, the least in the Kingdom is greater than John." (Matthew 11:11) He was the greatest of all. He was pure beyond measure, doing violence to his appetites. In his own mind he was a just and noble man, but "the least in the kingdom is greater than he," because he represents the external world.

We are told Elijah was John, who was Elijah-come-again. Well, Elijah clothed himself with the camel's hair, and he, too, wore the girdle of leather, for he represents that state of mind. And you'll find people in the world who are trying to get into the kingdom by doing violence to their appetites. They are strict vegetarians. They are strict this, strict that, and they really feel they should become a celibate or should order themselves so that they will not become disturbed, as so many priests have done - and that means that they are now pure people. Pure nothing.

In this world of ours, live a noble life in the garment that God gave you. Whatever it is, live it. And in your mind's eye, appropriate all the lovely things in the world. You have to pay rent, you have to buy clothes, to buy food; and if you get married and have a family, they are your responsibility while they are young. All right - all that is yours. There's no need to blame anyone if you don't have enough. Appropriate it, for all the states exist now. But where? They all exist in your own wonderful, human imagination. And all you do is adjust. Well, where do you go to adjust?

Standing just where you are, you adjust. Wherever you are, you adjust to the state desired. So, he's riding home in his car and money is falling on him - gently falling, green money - and then in a matter of moments he gets a raise. Why did that man have the impulse to give him a ten per cent raise? Because he appropriated it. You can work for a firm, as you know, all your life and it would never occur to the boss to give you a raise. And going in and begging him for it isn't going to do it. You've got to appropriate it first, and then let him think that he initiated it and give it to you.

I had a mother who understood this law beautifully. My mother wanted to come to this country on a vacation, and she would appropriate it. She would actually…in those days you didn't buy dresses. You brought your dressmaker home and you selected the cloth and she would make you dresses. She had all her dresses made. My father was busy in the business world.

He knew nothing of this daily activity of my mother - having all these dresses made. And she appropriated the trip to New York City while physically she was in the little island of Barbados. Then my father would come home and say: "You know - I don't want you here. You don't look very well. You look tired, and so I've just booked you for New York City, and you are sailing next week. All you have to do now is go and get a visa, because you are sailing next week and you are going to be there 3 months."

She would protest: "Oh," she said, "No, Joseph, that's so expensive. You shouldn't do it." Well, she already did it! She knew exactly what she was doing, but he wanted that feeling of one who was being generous, and she knew that he was the man of the house and if he did all these lovely things for her it would be nicer - it would make him feel that he was so generous. And so she pleased him by protesting, when in her heart of hearts she knew exactly what she was doing.

So I say: Do it all in your wonderful imagination. She would not have done it, if for one moment she thought he couldn't afford it, because she loved him and she loved the children she bore him. But why deprive him of the ability to do it or the desire to do it? Allow him full freedom to have the money to pay for it and the desire to do it. He could have had much more and not have the desire to do it. But she didn't argue with him. She simply appropriated the trip and "lived" in New York City. And as she did it, he had the brilliant idea to send her to New York City. And you wonder: How did it happen? It couldn't happen unless some one moved in imagination.

Whatever takes place is but movement within God, and God is your imagination! So you can move from one state to another in the twinkling of an eye. You don't need to sit down and burst a blood vessel; you simply do it in the twinkling of an eye. And if you do it with acceptance - with complete acceptance, no doubt as to your imagination's ability to externalize it - it will externalize it. As we told you last night, the definition of faith is simply the subjective appropriation of the objective hope. You appropriate it subjectively and then it becomes the objective fact. So, these are the stories told us in Scripture.

When Chambers said: *"It takes great imagination to follow Jesus Christ, and I, for one, have been lacking in such imagination"*, he was right in spite of his own position in his own town, a French town. And he made his exit from this world as a young man. Many of the great liberals of the world already quote him, but they will not quote that passage from his works, that he was inadequate to follow the mystery of Jesus Christ.

It takes a great imagination to follow him, because Jesus Christ is your imagination, not something external to you. He's in you. "Do you not realize that Jesus Christ is in you?" is what we are asked in Corinthians. (II Corinthians 13:5) Do you not know it? As though it would have changed!

Man, whose life is Jesus Christ, doesn't even know the source of his own life, that the foundation of his own being is Jesus Christ. That's the reality of man. And he doesn't know that reality. Well, I'll tell you who he is: his own wonderful, human imagination. And you accept it, and you will know all these mansions are only states of consciousness. They are all states of consciousness. Now, when you go into any state and dwell in it and return to it often in the course of a day, you are dwelling in it, and you will find yourself dwelling there, not only for today, but it will become a habit. And as it becomes a habit, it becomes externalized, and that's the world.

That then becomes your Esau. That then becomes your reality. That becomes the stronger of the two sons. It was once the weak one, and the minute you clothe him with reality and he becomes real, then you may forget it. As it becomes real, you may forget that that was once only a subjective state. As it takes on now objective tones, you may not remember how you got out of the former state into this if you desire it and never despair, for we started with the statement: "Let not your heart be troubled." (John 14:1) Quite often you will find these words appearing in different - as we say - guise: "Be not afraid"; "Fear not"; "Be not troubled"; "Be not anxious."

If you could remove fear from that, you remove all the titles of the world. If you are not afraid (and they couldn't make you afraid; if you know who God is, they can't make you afraid) - if you know who you really are, no man can make you afraid. For within you the power of powers is present, and that power is Jesus Christ. Is he not described in Scripture as the "power of God," in the very first chapter of I Corinthians? "Christ, the power of God and the wisdom of God." (I Corinthians 1:24) Paul saw no other. He only saw the power of God and the wisdom of God. As the poet said:

From the first - Power One -
I knew. Life has taught me
That; but for a closer view
Love were as close as He.

Yes, this I knew: "Power One". That I knew, and in my own vision, I can tell you, they come together. When love embraced me, there was man - infinite love as man. When I was commissioned and sent into this world to tell the story, it was power that sent me. But your being, your imagination, is a protean being. It can assume any shape, any form, in the twinkling of an eye. So the one who embraced me as love was the very one who sent me, but when he sent me, he wore the garb of might. He wore the garb of power.

His first revelation to man was as power: El Shaddai, God Almighty. He said: "I made myself known unto Abraham, to Isaac, and to Jacob as El Shaddai, God Almighty; but unto you, I have made myself known as I Am." (Exodus 6:3) Then, in the end, he makes himself known as the Father. But he first reveals his nature as power, and that's what he was when I was sent. I looked into his eyes and he didn't move his throat - didn't move his lips - but I heard every word that he thought as he looked into my eyes.

He looked into my eyes and thought, and his thought was: "Time to act." And then with these words: "Time to act," I was whirled out of that wonderful assembly and back upon my bed in this little garment of flesh, with these words ringing in my ear. But it was infinite might that sent me and yet infinite might was God Almighty, who was one with the infinite love who embraced me. But he did not command me as love; he commanded me as power. And so it is the same being; he is a protean being.

Proteus is simply the mythological god in the service of Neptune, who could assume any shape that would serve the purpose of Neptune. He could be a fish; he could be anything, if it served Neptune. And so he could assume anything, as you do in a dream. How do you manufacture all the symbolism of a dream? That's you! You are assuming all these wonderful symbols, all the images of a dream. It's yourself doing it; and you are clothing yourself in all the symbolism - whether it be animals, the fish, different names, or even of a different sex, because you are protean and you can clothe yourself in anything in the world.

But in my own case, it was power that commanded me, and I can still hear the words ringing in my ear - and yet I can see before my eyes infinite love that embraced me. When I fused, I fused - not with power, I fused with love, one with him, and I've never been separated from that power that is love - never! When I feel myself, it is always that same being that I saw. And I am quite sure that anyone who could see (not through mortal eyes, but through the awakened eyes of the risen Lord) would see that being as he looked at me, because he who becomes one spirit with the Lord becomes one body, becomes one spirit.

He who is united with the Lord becomes one spirit with him, and there is no divorce or separation from that moment on. But that body that he wears in the spiritual world cannot be seen by mortal eyes. Yet I can feel it and sense it and know what it is, but it's not this garment [indicating the body]. This little garment will slowly wither away and depart this little life, but he within me, who now wears it, will be that being with whom I fused back in 1959, for here in my wonderful world are unnumbered mansions.

So you don't have to condemn anyone who is in a state that he finds difficult to divorce himself from. Tell him how to do it. Teach him how to do it. Don't sympathize with him, because if you sympathize with him, you are fixing that state all the more; but tell him how to get out of the state. It is only a state!

Whether he be just or wicked, he's only in a state, and if you could only take the so called wicked man and persuade yourself that he is now a generous, kind, wonderful person, he would have a change of heart and not know why he has it. Something will happen within him, and he will become the kind and generous person that you have imagined him to be. If you want him to be that kind of a person, imagine him to be it, and persuade yourself of the reality of your own imaginary act, and he will conform to it.

My wife - back in 1945, when she left the Music Hall (she worked at the Music Hall for eleven years as a costume designer, and the head producer used to treat her unmercifully), I told her one day: "Darling, he couldn't do anything for you unless you allowed it. You actually feel that he is no earthly good. You feel that you are a cultured American lady. You went to Smith College. You were born and raised in a lovely environment. You never heard unkind things in your home. You never saw anything that was cheap. Your mother had lovely taste, beautiful things."

The interior was a beautiful, a huge, enormous home, with eight fireplaces, with every floor beautifully furnished, and she was raised in that environment. She went only to private schools, then off to Smith College, and then she worked in the Music Hall. Well, her father was managing director of the Music Hall, so when she went in there, she did not ask any favors because of her father's position, and this man simply lorded it over her.

She would say within herself (this she confessed to me): "Oh, you foreigner!" because he came from Russia. And she mentally would remind him that she is an American by birth for at least six or seven generations, and he came from Russia, and is now acting this way. Well, that's wrong. Whether he be a Russian or American, or English, or anything else, we are all one.

"Now, stop it, and allow him to praise you for your work. He's always condemning and always criticizing. Walk to work. You only walk five blocks from where you live to the Music Hall. Just imagine that he is not only praising you for your work, but he wants to use all of your designs, and the budget will not allow it, so he goes to your father and asks your father to increase the budget, that he may be allowed to use all the designs.

Your father's a businessman, and he's not going to do it. He's going to cater neither to you nor to him, but he has to run that at a profit for the Rockefellers. So, let him do it. But in your imagination assume that he does!" How long do you think it took for him to actually change his attitude towards her? I'll tell you: twenty-four hours!

When she came downstairs with this wonderful collection of designs, he raved about them, and he actually went to her father and begged him to increase the budget, that he may use them all. Her father would not allow it. And from that day on, he changed his attitude toward her radically for the better. Why? Because she changed hers towards him.

Are we not told in Scripture: "We love Him because He first loved us"? (1 John 4:19) You want to be quite fair? Well, start it here. Start it in your own imagination, and you'll find it responding on the outside, for the outer world only reflects the inner world. Start it there first, or you will never see it in the outer world! So, as she walked the street she simply imagined he walked with her, praising her for the work that she had done. And in 24 hours he praised her, and hoped her father would increase the budget, that he could use all of them. And then she retired.

And after she retired in 1946, he begged her to come back and do special shows. She went back and I think she did about six special shows for him. Who would have dreamt that he would ever ask her to come back and do one, after the treatment that she received? She has overcome it; completely overcome it. She knows that it is all within her. She doesn't turn to anyone to blame; she knows it's within her. She tries to find out where, in her, she's been carrying on these unlovely conversations, and then - changing the conversations within her - she changes the world in which she lives.

So, "in my Father's house," (which is your Father's house, for we have but one Father and we are that Father) are the unnumbered states of consciousness - and they dwell in the Father, and the Father is our own wonderful human imagination. The adjustment is made wherever you are. If you are off to bed, just about to retire, make the adjustment there. If you are sitting in a cocktail lounge, make the adjustment there. It doesn't matter where you are; you can do it within your imagination in the twinkling of an eye. What would it feel like if... and set your frame of reference. Your frame of reference... every one has a frame of reference.

Go down to the street tonight where people are lying in the gutter, and they have a frame of reference. They know what their parents or their friends think of them. They would know now what the same people would think of them, if they saw them differently.

If they only knew that within their mind's eye they could appear to themselves as one of the dignified beings pulling their own weight in this world (and their parents would be proud of them and not ashamed of them) and persuade themselves as they drop off into sleep that is how they are appearing to Caesar - they will rise from that gutter and be disgusted with themselves and the gutter and the environment, and go right on - go right up and do something that is worthy of a real man of this world. They would!

But who is going to reach them to tell them it's all within them? You can tell them because you know it. Don't go out and talk about it, but you'll have an occasion to turn someone from that state into another state - and you will find yourself knowing they are only states - and it's so easy to forgive one, knowing it's only a state. You will pull him out of the state because you learn to discriminate between the man and his present state. The present state may be most unlovely, but it's only a state; so instead of condemning the man, it's the state. You take him out of that state. He's the same being. The man who is rich today but formerly was poor - it's the same being.

The state of poverty did not vanish because he left it. It remains a state for anyone to fall into. And you move him into a state of wealth. Well, the state of wealth is a reality. It's fixed forever, and the day that he moves into it he's going to become wealthy, and no power in the world is going to stop him. As long as he remains in the state of wealth he'll reproduce it over and over and over, and you can't take it from him. If he doesn't know it's a state and he loses it all (he might not know it was only a state) and he'll remain out of that state in a state of poverty. But if he knows it was a state to begin with, he can always go back into that state. Any man can do it.

So, you know that it's a simple, simple technique, but you cannot be sure that you have moved unless you can see motion relative to a fixed object - some other object. You always have faces in your mind's eye of those who know you. How do they know you? If you like it, that's fine, if you don't like it, how would you like them to know you? Well then, you name it and then let them know you. All you do is: "Let there be light." (Genesis 1:3)

Let the face become luminous, reflecting that thing in you. As it is changed in you, you'll see it on their faces. Believe it! Believe in the reality of this subjective state. That is your hope, and this is the subjective appropriation of this hope. What hope? The faces are reflecting what you really want to see. And in a way that no one knows, you will become that man, and these faces actually will appear just as you have seen them in your mind's eye. And they will be proud of you, as you are proud of yourself.

Two

The Law

The whole vast world is no more than man's imagining pushed out. I must qualify that by saying that the world outside of man is dead, but Man is a living soul, and it responds to man, yet man is sound asleep and does not know it.

The Lord God placed man in a profound sleep, and as he sleeps the world responds as in a dream, for Man does not know he is asleep, and then he moves from a state of sleep where he is only a living soul to an awakened state where he is a life-giving Spirit. And now he can himself create, for everything is responding to an activity in man which is Imagination.

"The eternal body of man is all imagination; that is God himself." (William Blake)

Three wonderful case histories were given to me last Tuesday and I can best describe what I mean by telling you of one of them. Here is this lady driving east on Sunset and she comes to a stop at Laurel Canyon. A bus is to her right, and then she sees this little elderly lady in grey who is running diagonally across the street through traffic, trying to catch that bus. The bus driver sees her but he pulls out leaving her on the street.

The lady, who gave me this story, told me that she felt compassion for this elderly lady, but she was not in a lane where she could give her a lift; she had to pull out with her line when the light changed. She said to herself, "I will give that lady a lift just the same." So in imagination, she opens her car door and lets her in. Then still in her Imagination, she hears the lady tell her that she is meeting some friends a few blocks away and if she had to wait for another bus she is afraid they would not wait for her.

The lady in the car carried on this imaginary conversation and it took maybe a half a minute until she felt satisfied about it. Four blocks ahead, as she again stopped for a light, someone tapped on the car window, and here stands a breathless little elderly with gray hair dressed in gray. My friend lowered the window and the little lady said "I have missed my bus. Can you give me a lift? Friends are waiting for me and when they see I do not get off the bus they may go on and leave me."

My friend let her get into the car and then six blocks further the little lady said. "There are my friends!" and thanks the driver and gets out. Now here is a lady whom I say is awake. And may I tell you that in Heaven there was joy because one called a sinner (we are all sinners, for we are all missing the mark, and the mark is to awaken) has discovered that the whole world is responsive to what we are thinking. She could not actually give the first little lady a lift so she did it in Imagination, and then she sees this other elderly lady and gives her a lift.

Here she is enacting her imaginary drama, and four blocks later when the dream is completed this little ole lady taps at her car window. In her imagination she gave a lift to a little grey haired lady dressed in gray. Does it matter if it was the lady behind at the last bus stop or this lady dressed in gray? Everyone is responding to what we are doing in our imagination. There is no outside world that is really alive. It depends, for its aliveness, on the activity of man who is a living soul.

Man named the animals, the birds, the trees, - everything. God became man as a living soul, but He had to forget He was God to become man, and now man has to become a life-giving spirit, where he knows that everything is an imaginal activity. Here, at that corner where the first part of this little drama took place, half of those who witnessed it would bawl out the bus driver for not waiting for the old lady, and the other half would say she was a fool for running into the street.

This lady in the car could have reacted like that, for the dreamer does not know that he is dreaming. It is only when we awake they know they are causing the dream, or even had a dream. The lady in the car saw only someone who had failed to realize an objective, so she enacted a scene for her, implying she had realized it. And four blocks later she meets a little old lady who says to her the exact words she had heard in her Imagination. Her Imaginary dream unfolds in detail. An awakened dream is crystallized in the world.

"Real are the dreams of gods, as they slowly pass their pleasure in a long immortal dream."

When man completely awakens he dreams his pleasure and everything responds while he dreams it. We think everything in the world is completely independent from our perception of it, but the whole thing is dead. I see it, and come upon it, but the whole thing is dead.... frozen. Then I start an activity within me and then the world that was dead becomes alive, but not knowing I am doing it, I am sound asleep and then the whole thing takes over and it becomes a nightmare. But I must keep control and know it is dependent on me.

The world is infinite response and the thing that makes it alive is the living soul called generic man (male-female). And then God wove Himself into the brain of this generic man, and then He sleeps. As man begins to awaken he controls and takes over, and is no longer a victim of his vision, so he has control of his attention. Everyone is free to create his world as he wants it - if he knows that the whole thing is responding to him.

In Luke 13 we are told the story of five Galileans who have been murdered by Pilate. "And he mixed their blood with their offering, etc." And the central figure of the gospels which is your awakened imagination says to his followers; "Do you think these five were worse sinners than the others? I tell you 'No'. But unless you repent you will all likewise perish in the same manner." Here on one level we think it served them right, just as those who saw the scene on the Sunset Blvd would say "It served her right - cutting across the street like that!"

In this story in Luke we are told that a man sinned in the past and was murdered by Pilate. It has **nothing** to do with it. Then Jesus asked them, "Do you think that the eighteen upon whom the tower in Siloam fell and killed them were worse offenders than the others who dwell in Jerusalem? I tell you, No; but unless you repent you will all likewise perish.

On this level of the dream people think of getting even. It is a dream of confusion and people are reactivating, but man has to awaken and become an actor. On this present level man is always reflecting life, not knowing he is the cause of all he observes. But when he awakens from the dream and then becomes an actor. What percentage would have done what this lady in the car did? They would have reacted, or feasted on the fruit of the tree of good and evil.

They would have had a violent reaction, and then they would have had a violent resistance from this dead universe. But this lady makes her dream and the whole thing comes to pass exactly as she pictured it, even to the number of blocks. You might almost think she had manufactured that little old lady in gray, but I tell you everything comes in response to our own wonderful imaginal activity.

You can be anything in this world, but you cannot know it or expect it to come *unless* you act. If you react based on the past, you continue in the same pattern. To be the man you desire to be you must create the scene, as this lady did, and the whole world will be convulsed if that is necessary to bring it to pass. There is no other power but God, but God had to "forget" he was God in this state of sleep, and then He awakens and consciously determines the conditions he wants in the world.

So again I say to this lady, the angels rejoiced over your awakening, and - I say this without pride - they also rejoiced because I kept my promise that I would come and awaken this sleeper in the world of men. For I, also, had to forget everything to become man. For when one goes and then returns he has to forget everything to become man. For when one goes, and then returns he has to forget everything, but he promises he will carry out his pledge and help man awaken. Then the living soul becomes a life-giving spirit, and then creates.

Take it seriously. Do not go through this with your dream un-acted. It took this lady 30 seconds to enact her drama and another 60 seconds to realize it. You tell yourselves - it must take time- What time? Read Corinthians 1:18, I could go before men with all the words of wisdom, but know only one thing, the cross. To the wise it is foolishness, etc.

What is the cross? Think of it in this light. You began, seemingly in your mother's womb and end in the grave. You do not, but you have that picture. Look on the horizontal line of the cross as time. Intersecting this vertical line and call that infinite states, like Jacobs ladder. At any section of time I can move up or down. Time is flowing and the state with which I am identified still unfolds.

So, while seated in my car I can move up and enact a drama. I acted and remained within that state. It unfolded. It took 60 seconds. There are infinite states intersecting the line of time. We become one with a certain state and it demonstrates itself in actual phenomena. Everyone here, it need not take you more than 30 seconds to bring about a change of state. What would it be like? And you name your desire. Remain in that state, and that state, by the passage of time, will unfold in your world.

You do nothing about it once you have entered the state...for the outer must move by compulsion of the inner power. This little lady in gray had to come to my friend's car. Every detail of that imaginary act took place. Why not? The universe is infinite response. When you know that there is no one in the whole world could ever faze you, because he is a shadow.

I have seen the whole world dead, completely frozen, and then I allowed something within me to start and everything became animated. Then you ask yourself a million questions. Who am I? What is it all about? Why? Everything here is responding to the imaginal activity within man. When someone who is sick becomes well: when someone who is blind then sees, is that more of a miracle than what this lady told? She is awake. If you make a fortune it means nothing.

All the honors of men in a state of sleep are as nothing. You must "repent". It has nothing to do with the so-called judgment of God. It is only a dream and man is reacting to the dream and he does not know that he is the dreamer and causing all the dream. The literal meaning of the Greek word translated as repent means "a change of mind." It has nothing to do with the moral picture. The churches introduced that, but it has nothing to do with it.

I don't care what a man has done, if he changes his mind in this meaning of the word "repent" things will change, for he is then on the line of vertical line of states. He stands at a point on the states. There are infinite states and we must learn to distinguish between the state and the individual occupying the state. But I can now change and move into another state. I can in Time, do it in a split second and rise on the vertical line of the states.

So, "I come, only to teach the cross.", said Paul. I will rise within myself and ignore the former state, and within myself I will assume that things are as I want them to be. If I remain faithful, the passage of time will unfold it. So, Blake said, *"Eternity is in love with the productions of time."* I tell you, do not let anyone ever convince you that because of your past accomplishments or your present state in the world that you cannot change your position by rising within yourself, and then see the whole world respond. And I mean NOW!

So, I tell you this lady is awake; the Child is awake in her, the purpose of life is to awake. If the whole vast world or sleeping humanity thought her important, would she feel flattered? If in a dream everyone praised you and then you awoke and found it was all a dream, would you be flattered? One dreamer puts a medal on another dreamer, and they do not know it. It is only the awakening that is important.

Awakening and doing the will of God. God's will is in you active as your own Imagination, and His will is to realize the imaginal state. To realize something novel as this lady did or to maintain something to maintain in being, or to let things go that you feel are unlovely. I will do it all and only act, and stop re-acting. Then the whole book, The Bible, becomes alive. Leave all the "wise men to mock it or tolerate". Let them reach the moon or the stars, they are all dead. Nothing lives outside of man.

Man is the living soul, turning slowly into a life-giving Spirit. But you cannot tell it except in a parable or metaphor to excite the mind of man to get him to go out and prove it. Leave the good and evil and eat of the Tree of Life. Nothing in the world is untrue if you want it to be true. You are the truth of everything that you perceive. "I am the truth, and the way, the life revealed."

If I have physically nothing in my pocket, then in imagination I have MUCH. But that is a lie based on fact, but truth is based on the intensity of my imagination and then I will create it in my world. Should I accept facts and use them as to what I should imagine? No. It is told us in the story of the fig tree. It did not bear for three years. One said, "Cut it down, and throw it away." But the keeper of the vineyard pleaded NO"! Who is the tree? I am the tree; you are the tree.

We bear or we do not. But the Keeper said he would dig around the tree and feed it - or manure it, as we would say today - and see if it will not bear. Well I do that here every week and try to get the tree (you/me) to bear. You should bear whatever you desire. If you want to be happily married, you should be. The world is only response. If you want money, get it. Everything is a dream anyway.

When you awake and know what you are creating and that you are creating it that is a different thing. The greatest book is the Bible, but it has been taken from a moral basis and it is all weeping and tears. It seems almost ruthless as given to us in the Gospel, if taken literally. The New Testament interprets the Old Testament, and it has nothing to do with morals.

You change your mind and stay in that changed state until it unfolds. Man thinks he has to work himself out of something, but it is God asleep in you as a living soul, and then we are reborn as a life-giving spirit. We do it here in this little classroom called Earth or beyond the grave, for you cannot die. You can be just as asleep beyond the grave. I meet them constantly, and they are just like this. Same loves and same hates. No change. They will go through it until they finally awake, until they cease to re-act and begin to act.

Do not take this story lightly which I have told you tonight. Take it to heart. Tonight when you are driving home enact a scene. No matter what it is. Forget good and evil. Enact a scene that implies you have what you desire, and to the degree that you are faithful to that state, it will unfold in your world and no power can stop it, for there is no other power.

Nothing is independent of your perception of it, and this goes for that great philosopher among us who is still claiming that everything is independent of the perceiver, but that the perceiver has certain powers. It is not so. Nothing is independent of the perceiver. Everything is "burned up" when I cease to behold it. It may exist for another, but not for me.

Let us make our dream a noble one, for the world is infinite response to you: the being you want to be.

Three

The Hidden Secret of God

The mysteries of God are mysterious in character, yet they are proclaimed to all who can understand them. Paul, in his first letter to the Corinthians [as read in the second chapter of First Corinthians], is telling them a story so that their faith may not rest in the wisdom of men, but in the power of God. Now, he speaks of a different wisdom altogether.

He said: "Yet, among the mature, we teach wisdom. It is not a wisdom of this age or of the rulers of this age, for they are doomed to pass away." (I Corinthians 2:6) He speaks of an entirely different wisdom that he claims to be the secret - "the hidden secret of God, which God decreed before the ages for our glorification." (I Corinthians 2:7) Then he said: "For what person knows the thoughts of a man except the spirit of the man which dwells in him? So also, no one comprehends the thoughts of God except the Spirit of God." (I Corinthians 2:11)

Now we are told: after the Resurrection, those who are closest to him still did not understand him. For when he appeared, they said, "Lord, will you now at this time, restore the kingdom to Israel?" And he said to them, "It is not for you to know times and seasons which the Father has fixed by His own authority. But you wait until you receive the power which will come upon you when the Holy Spirit comes upon you."

That is the power of which I speak - when the Holy Spirit comes upon you. And then, with that power, you will be my witnesses, witnessing in Jerusalem and in all Judea and Samaria to the ends of the earth; but not until it comes upon you. And when it comes upon you, you are told, the

Holy Spirit is one's remembrance. "He will bring to your remembrance all the things that I have told you." The whole will come back, and then you will actually reproduce within yourself my story; that's what he is telling them.

He now disappears. He has now revealed to them the true Exodus: that the Exodus of the Old Testament was an adumbration - a foreshadowing. Resurrection followed by the "birth from above" is the true "Exodus" from this world of tears; this world of bondage. So, the Jews celebrate the Exodus, and they are still in bondage. And the Christians celebrate the Resurrection, and they haven't yet been resurrected. That whole thing is a drama.

When the Spirit comes upon you, which is the spirit of power, then "he will bring to your remembrance all that I have told you, which I have received from my Father." So within the individual upon whom this power comes, which is the Holy Spirit, the whole thing will unfold within him.

They completely misunderstood it, and they thought the restoration of a national theocracy was what was intended with the coming of Messiah. They did not realize that the truest coming of Jesus was the manifest power of the Holy Spirit; that when this power comes, it lifts you up from *within* yourself. And then, *you* actually are the Being that the world yesterday celebrated about his Resurrection. *You* are that One spoken of in Scripture. But you will not know it and be a witness to this until the power comes upon you. And that power is the power of the Holy Spirit. Then the whole thing unfolds within you.

Now you have heard of the story; we all know the story. Did you ever dwell upon the character called Judas? Today we speak of a man who is a betrayer of a trust. He is "a Judas". He simply betrayed the trust - any kind of a trust. A man just died in New York City in prison who betrayed the trust of the mafia. He was one of the leaders in the mafia, and gave to the FBI the true name ("Our Thing") - Cosa Nostra.

No one claimed his body. There he was; he died in prison because there was a price on his head - a fabulous price to kill him. So he was protected while he was in prison because he had revealed the secret of this thing that wormed its way into society called "Our Thing", where they made billions that you could not put a finger on it, and therefore wasn't taxable. But he betrayed it; so he was a "Judas".

Well, that is not the Judas of scripture. But who is this Judas? We are told that at the Last Supper, he said, "The one to whom I will give the sop, for my time has come." Everything was done on order in the Gospel of John. He never moved. He resisted all action until the right moment. "My time has not yet come", beginning with the second chapter. He said to the brothers in the seventh chapter, "My hour has not yet come."

He goes through the entire book stating that the time has not yet come. He is following a divine plan. So here we find predestination in one, and we find free will both joined together in man. He teaches man to exercise free will, and shows them how to change the pattern of life. But, he is under compulsion to fulfill the Father's will. Everything must be done on time. So, the moment of betrayal has come.

In the Eastern custom, two would sit on a divan or couch. The honored guest was always the one to whom the host gave the sop. He would take the sop, dip it into the dish, and then hand it to the honored guest. So: "The one to whom I give it, he will betray me." He turns and gives it to Judas, and Judas goes out quickly. And he said to him, "What you have to do, do quickly." It is perfectly told, may I tell you? I know from experience. "What you have to do, do quickly." And Judas goes out. Yet they do not understand who it is going to be who will betray him.

"Lord, is it I?"
"Lord, is it I?"
"Lord, is it I?"

Well, it is obviously the one to whom he gave it. Who then, is Judas? He betrays the Messianic secret. Now, "No one knows the thoughts of God, but the Spirit of God." Is he not, then, the Spirit of God? If he betrays God, only the Spirit of God could betray God, "for no man knows the thoughts of a man but the spirit of man, which dwells in him, and no one knows or comprehends the thoughts of God but the Spirit of God." Then, is he not the Spirit of God? For, no one can betray me but the spirit of myself!

Now we are told there are two traditions as to his "death" in Scripture. Matthew tells it in the 27th chapter that he went out and hung himself. In other words, he committed suicide. Jesus is made to say, "No one takes away my life. I lay it down myself. I have the power to lay it down and the power to take it up again." So here we find the suicide - the parallel. But in the book of Acts, it is said "He swelled up; and swelling up, he burst in the middle. Then all of his bowels came gushing out." (Acts 2:28) They were two entirely different traditions: one given to us by Luke, for Luke wrote the Book of Acts...and then we have the one in Matthew.

Now a friend of mine, he said:

"This happened to me a year ago. I didn't tell it because I didn't know, it seemed so strange to me. But this weekend, I was reading the 13th chapter of the book of John, reading of the Last Supper, reading all about the sop. Reading of these things, I thought, 'What nonsense! They saw where he gave the sop - to whom he gave it. Why ask all these questions then - is it I; is it I? And then one even whispered asking him who it is.' The honored guest could not be across the street. The honored guest would be right next to him - the one whose head was on his bosom; and he dipped the sop he gave him and said 'What you have to do, do quickly.'"

Then he said:

"A year ago I had a vision; and in my vision I saw you dead. You were dead. You were dressed in white - radiant white - and your bowels were completely out. That was your death. Not understanding it, I hesitated to mention it, because it struck me at the time that that would be Judas. And so, I saw you dressed in radiant white, and you were dead. And your death was caused by the swelling and bursting of your midsection, and out came all of your bowels, gushing out."

Here was "Neville", and he was dead. He saw the perfect vision. I tell you, when it happens everything in you:

*"All you behold, though it **appears** without, it is within, in your own wonderful human imagination, of which this world of mortality is but a shadow."* (William Blake, from "Jerusalem")

So, all these characters are within himself! And the nearest to him is the Spirit of himself, which is Judas. The word "Judas" is the same as "Judah", the one mentioned in the genealogy. And speaking of the genealogy, "Jacob was the father of Judah and his brothers." (Matthew 1:2) It didn't mention the first three brothers. It never mentioned the first three; it jumps over them and goes to the fourth one, Judah. "Judah" means the "hand"; but it's the hand of God - the *power* of God. It's the creative power of God, the directive power of God that can fulfill His purpose. And His purpose is to give Himself to man.

The story of Jesus is the biography of God. That's God. Now, when that unfolds itself and man, God has succeeded in giving Himself to man. That man, then tells it.

So today here we single out an individual as though this thing happened on Earth. It didn't happen on earth. This is God's plan. It is all written in Scripture. When it happens in you, you read Scripture to find the parallel, but the whole thing is taking place in a supernatural world, all within you. "He speaks to man through the medium of dreams, but he **reveals** himself in vision." It is God unveiling Himself.

So one who comes into my world - and no one comes unless the Father within me calls him - he has a vision. He hesitated for quite a while to tell me because of the tradition concerning Judas. He was the one whose bowels, as he swelled up, burst in the middle. And all of his bowels gushed out. He was the one who betrayed the secret, as I betray it every time I take this platform.

I am telling you the secret of God every time I take this platform. I am playing the part of Judas every Monday and Friday night. I play it every time I talk to a friend. If they call me on the phone, I am betraying the secret. "I have come, not to abolish the law and the prophets, but to fulfill them." So, I tell you the Law. I reinterpret the Law psychologically, and tell you that:

"An assumption, though false, if persisted in will harden into fact." (Sir Anthony Eden)

2000 years ago, you heard that same statement told in this manner: "Whatever you desire, <u>*believe*</u> that you have received it, and you will." It's the same thing told in a more modern form. *The very same thing.* If you dare to assume this, that or the other, and persist in your assumption, it will harden into fact and project itself on the screen of space. That is the Law. It's psychological.

Now the prophets - they predicted the sufferings of the coming One, and told of the glory that would be His. First, he was chosen in Him before the foundation of the world. "Those whom he ***foreknew***, He also predestined to be conformed to the image of His Son; and those whom He ***predestined***, He also called; and those whom He ***called***, He also justified; and those whom He ***justified***, He also ***glorified***."

Well, you can't take these five terms and come to any other conclusion than predestination. That is the Spirit-in-man fulfilling the Will of God, leading that man up to God himself! For the story of the Gospel is God's biography. When that story unfolds itself in the individual in the first-person-singular and present-tense experience, now it's *his* biography.

If it's God's biography, and it is his experience, then who is he? He *is* that power. When that power comes upon him, he *is* power. And who is the power of God? Jesus Christ. "Christ - the power of God and the wisdom of God."

When someone, now, puts his or her hand to the plow, and turning back, render themselves unfit for the Kingdom of Heaven; but the One Who called him or her, will not allow him or her, to unfit themselves for that Kingdom. And so, if he appears to her or to him as sheer power, it is for a purpose.

As we are told, "If one will not believe, having been called and having been spoken to," as told us in the story of Gabriel (Luke 1:18-23): "And Gabriel came into the presence of Zechariah and told Zechariah that the Lord had sent him," and then told Zechariah of the coming of the birth of John. And he said, "How will I know this? I am an old man, and my wife is advanced in years." And the angel replied, "I am Gabriel. I stand in the presence of God," - that is: wherever the messenger is sent, God is with him, for the Sender and the "sent" are one. And the word "Gabriel" means either the "power" of God or the "man" of God. You can translate it either way.

So, now you want to sign? "Well, this shall be your sign: you should be silent and unable to speak until that day when this thing is fulfilled." And when he came out of the temple, he could not speak; and those who waited on the outside in prayer while he lit the incense on the inside were dumbfounded, because they knew something had happened when they saw him. He couldn't speak; he was 'dumb'.

Then, when the child was born, and then on the 8th day, which was the day now to be circumcised, they wanted to know what to name the child. And they thought certainly "Zechariah", after his father. And he made signs, for he could not speak, to bring him a tablet, so that he could write. And he wrote on the tablet, "His name is John." And as he wrote, "His name is John", the whole thing was fulfilled, his mouth was opened, his tongue was loosened, and then he spoke.

That was sheer power. "Christ is the power of God and the wisdom of God." But in this world of ours, when I am put into the place of playing such a part, in His infinite mercy He takes from my conscious, reasoning mind that individual act so that I am not left with it. That part I will play in the depths of my own being. I will play anything that my Father, who is one with my Self, commands me to play, that they who would now stray from the path will be brought back into it.

If that little thing was only for one moment that you are dumb, unable to speak - and here for one moment there was no speech; but I tell you, this play is the Eternal Play. It didn't close yesterday when the bowl overflowed and all of a sudden they came out; when they reinterpreted the entire story and called it "positive thinking" or "positive decisions", and all this nonsense. This is the eternal story.

Wait until you receive power from on high, for the power will come and you will be overcome with the Spirit - the Holy Spirit. And "when the Holy Spirit comes upon you, it will bring to your remembrance all that I have told you." And what have I told you? My life. I have told you exactly what happened to me supernaturally. That will then happen to you individually, and you will know that I told you the truth. That is the *eternal* story of the gospel.

So he said, "Among the mature, I too impart a wisdom; it is not the wisdom of this age or of the rulers of this age, for they are doomed to pass away. I impart a secret and hidden wisdom of God, which God decreed before the ages for our glorification." That's what he imparted.

Then he tells us in that same chapter, the second chapter of First Corinthians, how it's impossible for any person to know a man's thoughts, except the spirit of that man which dwells in him. And therefore, no one knows or comprehends the thoughts of God, *except* the Spirit of God. And so, he sends the Spirit upon you. The real coming of Jesus - the return of Jesus - in the truest sense, is simply the manifested power of the Holy Spirit. That's his "coming."

He can't come in any other way. He becomes invisible. He departs this world, and then sends the Holy Spirit. Well, the Holy Spirit comes like the wind, may I tell you? Just like the wind! And when you hear it, it is the most unearthly sound you have ever heard...but its wind. It possesses you, and then you wake. You wake to find yourself entombed. Then you come out of that tomb where you have been buried...and then everything - the entire story now - unfolds within you, scene after scene without any deviation: and that's the Being that you are. And when it happens, and it comes to the very end, you know Who-You-Are. You are God Himself!

You are the Power of God that is Jesus Christ - "the power of God and the wisdom of God." And now you know the true Exodus from bondage. What you read about in the Old Testament was only an adumbration; a foreshadowing; but when it happens to you, this is the true Exodus when you are set free. Set free, because you have found the Son. "If the Son sets you free, you are free indeed." And the Son stands before you, and you know exactly who he is, and he knows who you are.

So don't close the book and wait for a year. "Set your hope fully upon the Grace that is coming to you at the unveiling and the revelation of Christ *in* you." For that's where he is! He is all buried within you.

In the meanwhile, use the law psychologically. External observation means nothing. All the outside ceremonies mean nothing; absolutely nothing. "Down with the bluebloods!" - that was my command when I was "sent". It's all just church protocol. That's what it means: down with it *completely*. Pay no attention to it - even to the little simple things, which might be very pleasant. When you sit down to dine, and someone calls upon you to say grace: say grace. Don't be abusive about it; say it. But you know it means nothing. But do it, if you are called upon to do it.

We do not have it at my home. We sit down, and I thoroughly enjoy my meal that my wife prepared, and I thank her for preparing it. But if one calls upon you to do it, do it. But all outside ceremony means absolutely nothing. That was my command when I was "sent": "Down with the bluebloods"...down with all church protocol. So, the so-called washing of the feet of these twelve elderly men, and the so-called kissing of the feet: that's out! It hasn't a thing to do with real, true Christianity.

I tell you what it is from experience. He will wake within you, and then you will know every one of those Disciples - what aspect of your own being each represents. And that one who was closest to him, the one who was his friend, the one to whom he gave the honored piece: that was Judas, the "Hand" of God - the directive hand that could fulfill his purposed end by betraying the secret - as I do, every time I talk to you. I betray the secret of God. I can't betray it if I don't know it. No one can betray what he does not know. And so, one must first know it to betray it. But I *am* betraying it. I am telling you exactly how it happens, in the way that I have told you.

It will come suddenly upon you - the Holy Spirit. It will come like a storm wind; and when it comes, you will wake up to find yourself entombed, and then you will have the innate wisdom (for Christ is also the wisdom of God, not only the power of God) to move that stone from where it was. That was the "seal". Break it by pushing it from within. You will come out, and you will find surrounding you the witnesses to the Great Event that God succeeded in His purpose, which was **waking you as God**.

For this is the "birth" of God, "not born of blood or of the will of the flesh or the will of man; but of God." And you come out; and the sign of your "birth" is present, and here is the sign wrapped - as you were told - in swaddling clothes. You pick it up, and in the most endearing manner, you say: "How is my sweetheart?" And the whole thing vanishes, including the three who witnessed the birth.

Then comes the second Great Event, when he stands before you, and you fulfill Scripture, the 89th Psalm: "I have found David, and he has cried unto me, 'Thou art my Father, my God, and the Rock of my Salvation.'" And then he stands before you. And this relationship is forever. It's the returning memory, for you do not have the feeling that it happens now. It's simply that your memory has returned, just as though you had suffered from total amnesia. It's not something that startles you; you have always known he was your "son". That's the feeling that I had. So, all of a sudden, he comes back. What comes back? "The Holy Spirit is upon me." Well, *who* is the Holy Spirit? He "who brings to your remembrance all that I have told you."

"And did not David, in the spirit, call me 'my Lord'"? Well, when he calls you "my lord" - which is the name of my Father, for all sons called their father and spoke of their father as "my Lord" - so: "David, in the spirit, called me 'my Lord'". He does it *in spirit*, not here on Earth.

And then comes the grand severance of your body from top to bottom: and your ascent into heaven, separating the event called "Resurrection" from the "Ascension". And you can count them. It's not forty days. You can count the whole thing up. It's between...mine, for example, was on July 20th, 1959, and the ascent took place on April 8th, 1960; and that's when one ascends - ascends into heaven. And the whole thing, as you were told, reverberates like thunder.

And then comes the Seal of Approval on the twelve hundred and sixtieth day. And that is the descent of the Holy Spirit in bodily form as a dove. And here he rests upon you. You bring him up, and he is smothering you with kisses when the whole thing fades. And then you go tell it.

And so, the story of Judas; when he does betray, he does it quickly, I tell you. You are seated on the floor explaining the Word of God to those who are seated before you, and he is one of them. And suddenly, he jumps up...and you know exactly what he is going to do. He is going to tell you [you won't use the word "betray"] he is going to tell exactly what he heard you say: you are speaking of the Kingdom of God. And he is going to tell that you are speaking of the Kingdom, and that you are the King. And he is going to tell the authorities concerning what you said. He *has* to betray the Kingdom; so he goes out, and he tells it.

Then comes the "authority", and he unveils your arm, and his name who went out is the "Arm of God", the "Hand of God". He unveils it, and you see the relationship between the one who went out and yourself. Now you are completely unveiled when he nails into your shoulder that peg - that wooden peg and hammers it in, and then takes off the sleeve and takes the arm and it's bare. And then you know the 53rd chapter of Isaiah: "Who has believed our report, and to whom has the Arm of the Lord been revealed?" And as everything is placed upon that Being, he has then to bear the burden; but he will see the travail of his efforts - of his labor; and he will rejoice. He will be satisfied when he knows that he got through.

So you can say to anyone, if they see me in any role that seems a harsh role, then know that I consciously am not aware of it while I played that part. I have to play it, for this is a supernatural world of which I speak. It is a supernatural Being of which I speak. It's a supernatural part that I am playing when I play those parts at night. And certain parts, I am relieved of the memory of them, for they have to be done - to "jack one up" - "having put his hand to the plow and turning back, unfits himself for the Kingdom of Heaven." (Luke 9:62)

And what caused him to turn back? Doubt.

They questioned; and so when Zacharias asked "How will I know this? I'm an old man, and my wife is advanced in years. How could she conceive and bear a son?", he said: "I stand in the presence of God." In other words: I am speaking for the One who sent me, and He never left me. Therefore he stands with me. Now sheer power is going to make you dumb; and so he said to him: "You will be silent, unable to speak, until that which I have foretold has come to pass, because you did not believe the words that He gave me to speak. I spoke them, but you did not believe my words."

So, you will see me in many roles. Many of you *have* seen me in different roles. Yet my conscious, reasoning mind has always been removed on my return from certain parts that I had to play, for I am under compulsion to play those parts, after being awakened. And my friend had to see me in that role to know who Judas really is. And I *am* Judas every time I betray the Messianic secret; and I am the one who told him to do it quickly.

That scene I recall vividly. "What you have to do, do quickly." He certainly did it quickly. There was no time between his departure and the arrival of the authority who came in and severed my sleeve and hammered into my shoulder that wooden peg, on which he then placed the burden.

So I tell you: this play, is an eternal play. It goes on forever and forever and forever. And each one makes his exit - which is the Exodus - from this world of tears into a blissful state; but only in that way does he ever make the Exodus. So when they sing the hymns of how they were led out of bondage in Egypt into a world of freedom - and yet all are still as enslaved as they were thousands of years ago, then what are they commemorating? For when the real leader - the new Moses - comes, they would not recognize them.

The new Moses came and was called "Jesus", which means "Jehovah". God Himself came this time in the form of man. And that's the new Moses; and his life is the pattern that man will one day imitate - actually experience; and therefore, it's **his** pattern. It is his, and it's the only way you will ever make an exit from this world. "Death" will not take you out of this world. You will "die" and be restored to life just as you are now, in a world just like this. It's terrestrial, and you will still be making your effort as you do right now.

There is no transforming power whatsoever in the thing called "death". There is no transformation in death. You find yourself the same being young, yes. But that's not transformation - the same identity. But that of which I speak is a complete transfiguration - a complete transformation of form You are no longer this little garment You are glorified, and you "wear" a glorified body that doesn't have the needs of this body at all. And wherever you go clothed in that Body, everything is perfect. There is no place you could go. Walk through "hell", it will become heaven. And some one clothed in *these* garments, [i.e. the physical body], walking through heaven, would turn it into "hell".

So I tell you: you are in for the most glorious thing in the world. And what I have told you, I tell you from my own personal experience, I am not theorizing; I am not speculating. I knew that someone had to see me in that role. And he had this vision a year ago; but because of custom and his association with the idea of Judas as the one whose bowels came gushing out, he hesitated to share his story.

And loving me as he does, and believing me as he does, he didn't know how to associate that with the one that he so loves and trusts to tell the truth. Well, I can tell you, they are the same being, for he is the spirit of the one - the honored guest to whom he gave the sop. That is the honor to position, not around a table as we have it here in da Vinci's picture. There was no table; not in the Eastern world. You sat on a divan - not more than two at any one moment. And divans were around.

And the host, if he ever dipped it, would take a piece of meat and dip it; and the one whom he gave the meat or a piece of bread [that was the sop], the one to whom he gave it: *that* was the honored guest. As we today, sitting around the table, we seat the honored guest to our right; and here that is the honored position. But there, the one whose head was on his breast - and he just simply said, "Who is it?": who is nearest to you but your spirit? "So, no one knows or comprehends the thoughts of God but the Spirit of God."

So, if God was ever betrayed, he could only be betrayed by the Spirit of God. **It had to be revealed.** It could not be discovered by any philosophical reasoning. No man in this world, as you are told in Scripture: "man could not find God". All the wisdom of man could not find God. God had to reveal Himself, and the revealing *is* the betrayal of God. *He betrays himself by unveiling Himself to man.* And this is the story as it is written and told us in Scripture.

You set your hope fully upon that moment in time when it comes to you. It is called "Grace" in Scripture. "Set your hope fully upon the Grace that is coming to you at the revelation of Jesus Christ." Well, "Grace" is simply an unearned, unmerited gift of God to man. And that gift is God Himself. So you are raised from the level of being a son, to the level of being the Father.

Four

Grace vs Law

We are told in the first Chapter of John: "The Law was given through Moses, but grace and truth came through Jesus Christ." Unnumbered columns have been written about this grace vs. law. Tonight I am speaking not from theory. I am speaking from experience.

We are called on to pass on to other generations, succeeding generations, our testimony. We are told in the First Epistle of John 1:1-3: "That which was from the beginning, which we have heard, which we have seen with our eyes...that which we have seen and heard we proclaim also to you, so that you may have fellowship with us."

These are the two births that take place in every individual in the world. No one brings about his own physical birth. He is born by the action of powers not his own. And so, no one brings about his own spiritual birth. He is born by the action of powers beyond his own. The first - we admit we are here, clothed in this garment of flesh. We find ourselves here but we know we had not a thing to do about it. We simply found ourselves. You will find yourself born spiritually in the same miraculous manner. You will be born from above, just as you were born here from below. Then there will be God's mightiest act, and you will be begotten and born from above, by the action of powers not your own.

We turn first to the law. In the very beginning God established the law of identical harvest: "And let the earth put forth vegetation, trees yielding seed, and fruit trees bearing fruit, in which is their seed, each according to its own kind." Here we find that the harvest is nothing more than the multiplication of the identical seed. "Be not deceived, God is not mocked. Whatever a man sows so shall he reap." That is this world, this law. Tonight I will show you what I have found about this sowing.

Causation in our world is really mental. It was not always known as a mental state; it was believed (in the beginning) to be spiritual. And so laws were instituted and men abided by these laws. Outwardly they observed the laws. Then came the great revelation of "grace" that interpreted the law, thus bringing grace. For, says he: "Do not think that I have come to abolish the law and the prophets; I have come not to abolish them but to fulfill them." And then he interprets law for us and puts it on a mental plane. "You have heard it said by men of old, 'Thou shalt not'" and then he states it.

"But I say unto you," and then he puts it on an entirely different level and not one statement conveys it more graphically than this one: "You have heard it said of old 'Thou shalt not commit adultery, but I say unto you, to look on a woman lustfully is to already have committed the act with her in your heart.'" To restrain the impulse, that is not good enough; but not having the desire, for then you haven't committed the act. But to have the desire, and because of the consequences of your act you restrain the impulse, that is still not good enough - the act was committed with the impulse.

Here, we are on an entirely different level, a mental level, and this is what I have discovered about this level. I can stand here physically, and be in any part of this world mentally by assuming that I am there, then, viewing the world from that assumption rather than thinking of that state. Standing here, if I desire to be elsewhere, though at the moment my reason tells me I can't afford it, my senses tell me I haven't the time - you are committed, you will be here next Friday, you couldn't get there and be back so here you are stuck. Well,

I know from my own experience that if I dared to do it, though everything in this world would tie me here, there will be a reshuffling of the events of life and compel the journey on my part, and it worked. That assumption of mine would build a bridge of incidents across which I would move to the fulfillment of that state. No power in the world could stop it. I will walk across a series of events from the moment that I do it. Things would happen to compel me to go, and I, physically - the man - could not resist it. That would compel the journey.

Now the same thing is true not only of a physical journey, but a journey into other states - like wealth, faith, like anything in this world. Suppose at this moment I desired certain security that I do not now enjoy - I hunger for it. What would it now be like if I were in possession of security? Let me now make the same psychological motion - all in my imagination - and then view the world from that assumption, just as though it were true.

If I dare to assume that it is so - I can acquaint you with this law and then leave you to your choice and its consequences. Many a person who had nothing, who hungered for wealth, and they got it, but oh! what things happened to them when they got it! They wanted it and if you want it, take it. You can always give it up, but here is the law by which man moves in this world.

So, I will acquaint you with the law and show you how I operate it and how it works. But may I tell you: no matter how good you are in this world, no matter how wise you operate the law, it doesn't in any way qualify you for the second radical change in your mind, which is called "grace" - that is the second birth: the twice-born man has received "grace." And grace is God's gift of himself to man. That is grace.

No matter how wise you are, you are on a wheel with the first birth. Play it as wisely as you can, and I hope you will play it wisely when you hear the law and how to operate it. But it cannot in way qualify you for the second birth. That is grace, that is the gift, and you cannot bring that about anymore than you brought about the first.

Now the second birth is sheer fantasy. It is called, not salvation - grace is salvation. "What must I do?" they asked. For he made the statement: "What if you own the whole vast world and lose your life?" Then he said: "It is so much easier for a camel to go through the eye of a needle than a rich man to enter the Kingdom of God." And they said to him: "Well, then who can be saved?" He said: "With men it is impossible, but nothing is impossible to God."

With man, yes, it is impossible; he can't save himself. When man tells you he is a self-made man he is not speaking of any knowledge of this mystery. No self-made man. For this is the gift, the second is a complete gift. And what is the secret of God's election? I do not know, I can't tell you.

I can share with you what I have experienced and tell you how it comes. It is a process, something that happened so suddenly. It comes without warning - no one knows the moment it is going to come, and suddenly you are born. You are actually born. You are consciously born. I have no conscious memory of being born from my mother's womb, none whatsoever. I was born on a certain day of a certain month of a certain year, and on a certain little island in the West Indies.

I had no knowledge of it, and then gradually consciousness possessed me, and when I was four (or not quite four) I began to function consciously with memory - but memory didn't go back to my birth. But the second birth is something as though you were actually doing it yourself, and every moment of time is conscious and so vividly alive. The whole thing you are doing, and the very moment to the end of birth is taking place in you, and out of your own wonderful being you are coming, and until that moment you didn't know you were dead.

You took it for granted you were alive and that one day your body would die. And so, whether you survived or not, you didn't know, but that would be death and those who saw you put away, whether cremated or in the earth, they would speak of you as someone who was dead, but not while you walked the earth with them. And yet, there comes the moment in time when suddenly a power beyond your wildest dreams is taking place in you. And you aren't doing it, you have no control.

It is being done to you and as the power is intensified, you awake. And you always thought prior to that moment, you were awake, you were alive and walking about the earth. And here for the first time in eternity you are awakening in a tomb, and the tomb is your skull. And you find this being completely sealed and entombed in your own skull and you are fully awake for the first time in eternity.

Then begins the work and you come out as one being self-born, truly begotten by yourself, and out you come. The entire drama as described for us in the gospel you are enacting - you are being self-born. The witnesses become present and they are here to witness this event in eternity. They can't see you because you are invisible, but you are more real than they are, more real than anything in the world at that moment -and yet, you are invisible.

Then you know what it means: "God is Spirit and those who worship Him worship in spirit and in truth. And as God has life in himself - God the father - so now he grants the son to have life in himself." All of a sudden you awake, and the force - the intense power you feel coming from you that now seems to be in the corner of the room - is centered all over. All of a sudden it comes to the end and you return once more, fully clothed, in this simple little garment out of which you have just for a moment emerged. It is the most fantastic garment in the world.

That was grace but it comes in stages. It has three fantastic parts to it. That first one is simply your birth from above to fulfill the 3rd [chapter] of John: "You must be born from above, for unless you be born from above you cannot in anywise enter the Kingdom of Heaven," which fulfills that chapter. Then comes the second, when God really gives you himself. Suddenly a similar power possesses you and you can't stop it, not a thing you can do about it. Suddenly as you are tied with it, your whole being explodes, and here he presents you with his son.

Now the 17th verse of the 1st chapter of John, after you are told: "Grace and truth came through Jesus Christ" (we are told how it comes through Jesus Christ), we are told: "No man has ever seen the Father; the Son who is in the bosom of the Father, he has made him known." And you didn't know you contained within you the son of God, and suddenly there is an explosion and he is standing before you and he calls you "father."

You don't see yourself; he calls you "father" and you know he is your son. Here the father-son relationship is established forever. He calls you "father" to fulfill the 89th Psalm: "I have found David, my servant..." and he has "cried out to me 'Thou art my Father, my God, the Rock of my salvation'" - the fulfillment of the great messianic 89th Psalm. You look at him and there is no doubt in your mind who he is and there is no doubt in his mind who you are.

In the 3rd chapter of John, in the great gift, he explains: out of the blue you are torn in two from top to bottom and then you are sent, a living being, something that is fire and alive, and you ascend right into Zion, which is yourself. These three parts mark the great gift. No one in this world is good enough to earn it, therefore all will get it.

God actually expresses to man a mercy with which man is incapable, with his conscience, of ever judging himself as worthy of. No man in this world with conscience and mercy could ever judge himself as mercifully as God judges him.

So what man has done - I certainly have done it, you have done it, the whole vast world has done it, and we are so fearful while we are here in this world of law, of doing it - and in spite of our limitations, in spite of our weaknesses, God's infinite mercy brings about the second birth. And we are all taken up in this eternal place where we are put into the everlasting temple which God is making out of us, making out of himself. For he gives himself to man before man can be free to begin the everlasting temple.

No one can fill your place. No one can fill my place. Not one can be displaced. Not one in any way can be rubbed out. The temple will be unfinished. I know from my own experience not one can be unsaved, I don't care who he is, no matter what he has done in this world, everyone will be saved. What must I do to be saved? Believe the Gospel.

Now we are told we can delay it; that is why I find it difficult to believe that. Still, it is Scripture. Hebrews 4:2: "And the good news preached unto us was also preached unto them; but it did not benefit them, because it was not mixed with faith in the hearer." Tonight some of you could reject it, and that may appear on the surface to delay your call. It may, I do not know.

I have no assurance that you can delay it; but it would appear that rejection on the part of one - because he heard it but did not accept it, because it didn't make sense to him -though you reject it and maybe by your rejection delay your call, eventually you will be called, because he puts you through all the paces of the world until finally you have no power to reject the story when you hear it.

But while we are here in this world of law, let me now quote you the 1st Psalm. It is a marvelous benediction: "Blessed is the man who delights in the law of the Lord, who meditates on it day and night . . . for in all that he does, he prospers." "In all that he does," not a few things. And the law is so simple. If you go to the foundation it is mental, not physical. Go to church, as people who practice it outwardly thought would in some way bring good for them. That wasn't it. It's mental. Causation is mental, so the law is mental. Find the law: "Blessed is the man who delights in the law, mediating on it day and night, for in all that he does he prospers."

Walk now by faith, not by sight. Romans 17:4: "He calls a thing that is not seen as though it were seen and the unseen becomes seen." "For the things that are seen," we are told, "were made from things that do not appear." We see a man - well what made him what he is? He once assembled certain states and knowingly or unknowingly he fell into it, and falling into it he remained long enough to take on that initial statement of God: "All things must bring forth after their own kind." The law of identical harvest. The harvest is only the multiplication of the identical seed.

So I fall into a state. I do it wittingly or unwittingly, but I fall into a state. Remaining in the state, suddenly the stump comes out. Someone begins to appear in my world who is instrumental in making me move forward in the direction in which I should go. I may on reflection think he, the instrument that moved me forward by certain contacts, was the cause of my being forward. No, the cause was unseen.

As you are told: "Things seen were made by things that do not appear." He appears, so he can't be the cause. If that is true then I will thank him for what he did but I can't claim he was the cause of my good fortune, though he introduced me to the right people and all things added up to the thing that I was doing. But the cause of it all was my assumption and my faithfulness to that assumption.

So, I dare to assume that I am, or that you are what I would like you to be, and assuming that you are what I would like you to be, and feel that you would like to be it, I am unmoved in that assumption and you become it, without your knowledge or your consent. I don't need your consent or knowledge if causation is mental.

So I warn you of the law and leave you to your choice...and its risk, because you can use it unwisely. But my hands are now washed of that. I cannot stop it. I can't be like a mother over you, stating that you should not do this. As you are told in the Book of Deuteronomy: "I place before you this day good and evil, life and death, blessing and cursing; choose life." He suggests you choose life but he can't take from you the right, having set you free, to choose anything you want; it is all spread before you.

If you imagine something unlovely of another, he'll come to that. It will boomerang too, but it will come to pass, for you are entirely free to imagine anything in this world, for imagining creates reality. A man imagined - if he imagines it and persists in that imaginal act, it will come to pass. And that's the law.

If there were no other than the wise use of law - to own the whole vast world and yet not to be redeemed from that wheel of recurrence - this would become the most horrible hell in the world. Fortunately God started in the beginning a plan of redemption, and its grace, where he saved us from the wheel of recurrence. And what is his greatest secret, where he picks you at one moment of time, picks another at another moment of time to put him into that eternal structure, the everlasting temple not made with hands?

I do not know. I only know he promised us to build a temple for us, anonymous. We are the temple, "We are the temple of the living God," a temple in which God will dwell, and yet we are free beyond the wildest dream of man. For we are God himself in the spot we call the "New Jerusalem." So, here, use it wisely for yourself and for others. Every time you use your imagination lovingly on behalf of another you are literally mediating God to another.

Do it. But even if you are the most loving, the most generous, the kindest being in the world, you still cannot by your own effort be born from above. It is a gift, an unearned gift and you can't be good enough. To me that is the most exciting thought in the world, because no man can look me in the eye and tell me he feels himself worthy of such a birth. With a memory and a conscience he couldn't possibly do it. And yet with my memory of the past I would say: "Neville, you are unworthy of it." Therefore, because I know in my heart I am unworthy, I can say to every being in the world: you are going to get it.

If I felt I was worthy of it, then I would have to go out and try to make everyone good, as I conceived myself to be. But I don't conceive myself to be good, as the world calls good. I have done unnumbered things of which I would be ashamed, and still feel I am capable under stress of doing things of which I would be ashamed. And yet, I have had the grace of God, the second birth from above. I can't conceive of anything more encouraging in the world than to share with others your own experience and tell them that they cannot lift themselves by their own bootstraps.

This is an act of mercy, and mercy is God in expression because God is love and mercy is God in action. And the mightiest act of God is when you, the sound sleeper, he awakens and you don't know you are asleep. No child born of woman could cross the threshold that admits to conscious life without the death of God. He died to make me alive - the mystery of life through death, and then this mighty act of resurrecting himself as you. Then you know the mystery of the Epistle of John: "It does not yet appear what we shall be, but we know when he appears we shall be like him."

We shall be like him, for there is no change in your identity. All of a sudden you awaken to the full glory of your inheritance. You have inherited heaven, but the full glory of that inheritance is not fully realized in you - or for the moment is not fully grasped by you while you are still in this body. You must then play the part of the apostle, and share it with those who will listen to you, until that moment in time when he takes off the garment.

Then that which ascended is completely displayed to you and to the heavenly host, but you have played and shared with the others all that you have experienced. It is called the apostolic testament: "That which was from the beginning, that which we have heard and seen with our eyes. That which we have seen and heard we now proclaim unto you that you may share with us this fellowship." And then that fabulous passage that always closes the Anglican service (which in our country is the Episcopal service), Corinthians 13:14: "The grace of the Lord Jesus Christ and the love of God and the fellowship of the Holy Spirit be with you all."

What a benediction! What a benediction to say to a gathering like this: "That may the grace of the Lord Jesus Christ," (that is the second verse) "which comes from the love of God, that through whose birth you may have and share the fellowship of the Holy Spirit, and may he be with you all." That is how all Anglican services close, in the hope that someone, or maybe all, will in the not distant future share in that fellowship. To me it is the most inspiring just to read it and just try to feel it.

So Grace vs. Law is not really in conflict. For he said: "I have not come to abolish the law or the prophets but to fulfill them." Peter, in his first Epistle (1:10) identifies grace with salvation: "The prophets who prophesied of the grace that was to be yours searched and inquired about this salvation." So he associates grace with salvation. The minute it is given he is saved, he's been redeemed. But because no one can play your part, you will be redeemed.

Don't go back in memory and try to find other things you could undo towards salvation. Do that towards this world, to make yourself happier and free in this world, but not toward salvation. Because if it was not for God's infinite mercy to hide your past from you, you couldn't live with yourself. No man in this world could live with himself if he could now bring back into memory the past. He couldn't because you'll play all the parts. You have been a long, long time in coming and at the very end you will have played all the parts. Therefore, in the end you can say: "Father forgive them for they know not what they do."

There is a purpose to God's play, a fabulous purpose. As Blake said:

"Do not let yourself be intimidated by the horrors of the world. Everything is ordered and correct and must fulfill its destiny in order to achieve perfection."

So we have all played it. Had I not played all the horrible parts in the world I could not be merciful when I read about them in the papers. I could not in my heart feel that some mercy should be stressed nor have the impulse for mercy had I not played it. But in the end, having played all you will forgive all. And so, everything in the world, you'll have played all and therefore fitted yourself for God's use in the building of His temple.

I can't get away from a sense of predestination when I read Scripture. Romans 8:28-30: "We are called according to his purpose. For those whom he foreknew he also predestined to be conformed to the image of his son. And those whom he called he also justified; and those whom he justified he also glorified." You cannot take these five terms: foreknowledge, predestination, called, justified, and glorified, and interpret them in any way to avoid the conclusion of predestination. I don't see how you can. "You were with me in the foundation of time," you are told.

He called us in the beginning before the world was. And now he calls us according to his purpose when this section of his fabulous (you can't conceive of it) living structure is about to be completed. And only you can fit one portion of it, so he calls you. And the one he calls he has predestined, but he calls. And the one he calls he justifies. You can't be justified by your actions; he justifies you. And then he glorifies you. And glorification is the gift of himself as told us in John 17:5: "Father, glorify me with thine own self." So, he glorifies the individual with himself. The entire five terms leads to one conclusion of a predestined, foreknown state. He foreknew the entire thing and is building towards it.

Now the opposite of grace is disgrace. The Bible speaks of it as the "wrath of God," the "anger of God." We know what it is to be in disgrace. Grace is the unearned gift, the greatest thing in the world, the gift of God himself. And the opposite would be almost the absence of God. Jeremiah 23 makes this statement: "The anger of the Lord will not turn back until he has executed and accomplished the intents of his mind. In the latter days you will understand it clearly."

It seems that God has forsaken us when we go through a war, when we are going through some horrible disgrace where the world has collapsed upon us. A child has gone astray and society frowns upon us because we are the parents of that child. Or maybe my husband or wife has done something to disgrace the family, the community. God has forsaken us.

So I pass through the fires of affliction, these horrible fiery ordeals, displaced (the opposite of place) where once he was with me and guided me. But "He will not turn back until he has accomplished the intents of his mind. In the latter days you will understand it clearly." And you will forgive all and be happy that he in his infinite wisdom and mercy could put you through that fiery ordeal to bring you out qualified to fit in his eternal temple.

So no one will be condemned in the end. No one will be unsaved. When they ask you: "What must I do to be saved?" go to the Scripture and show that with man it isn't possible. (That is the 10th chapter of Mark, 26-27.) With man, no, it isn't possible, but with God all things are possible. They couldn't understand how a man could be saved after he told them what he had, about the camel and the rich man. The rich man does not necessarily mean a man with money.

The first Beatitude tells you: "Blessed are the poor in spirit for they shall receive the kingdom." The poor in spirit is the one who is not complacent. Not everyone who has money is complacent. You could be socially prominent and very complacent. You could be intellectually a star, have your PhD's or your degrees behind you, and you are above it all. You know everything because conferred upon you is the degree given by man. In this world of ours there is so much of real learned ignorance. I am not saying that all who have degrees are snobs.

You cannot by these earn the Kingdom, no matter what you do. For the "Wisdom of this world is foolishness in the eyes of God." Not a thing that man knows here through his efforts will in any way function where he is destined to be. For he is rising into a world that will be completely subject to his imaginative power. Everything in the world will be under His control. Because God - having given Himself to man - God being all-wise, He will be all-wise.

God being all-powerful, all-loving, He'll be all-powerful, all-loving, for He gives Himself to man. And so, you will not be replaced by anyone, and all will be equal in the eyes of God, because it is Himself. He can't be more than what He gave you. And one will not be greater because you can't get more than what God gave you, for He gave you Himself, as though there were no others in the world: just God and you. And finally: only you.

Five

Seedtime and Harvest

This chapter's subject is seedtime and harvest. Although it bears the same title as one of the author's previous books, it is not to be found in that book, for that book is an attempt to interpret some of the more difficult passages of the Bible. I have given you in those nine chapters a mystical view - and also direction on how you yourself may approach the interpretation of the Bible; for as you know, it is not a book of history. And so, when I became aware of deeper meanings in the passages than those normally assigned to them, I began to see them or to apprehend them mystically. And so I have given you a mystical interpretation of many of the darker passages.

For instance, when Solomon made himself a chariot of the wood of Lebanon, he made it himself; no one made it for him. That's what you must do. That's what I must do. That's what everyone must do.

And in that chapter, I showed you the wood is not wood, as you know wood. It means the wood of Lebanon is the incorruptible mind; but you make it for yourself. And we showed you the sides, what they were made of, and what the meanings really are. Then we took that very strange passage - the instruction to the Disciples to take off their shoes or provide no shoes when they travel, and we showed you the word "shoe" is not just the thing I wear on my foot. It is the symbol of the spirit of "let me do it for you".

For the shoe takes upon itself not only the dirt and the muck that would normally fall upon the wearer's foot, but it protects the wearer from any contact with the outer world, and so anyone who offers to do for us what we should do, and could do far better ourselves, is offering himself as our shoe, and if I would awaken spiritually I must do it for myself. I must take my own mind and control it - take my wonderful imagination and actually control it and set it to noble purposes, and not have some intermediary come between myself and God. For the God of this world is an internal God.

He is that inevitable force that expresses in outward facts the latent tendencies of the soul. And so, if I would discover that God, I cannot have you do my work for me. I cannot have you eat my spiritual food and expect to grow spiritually. So that is really the attempt of the nine chapters in the book "Seedtime and Harvest". But this particular subject - I want to approach it differently. This statement is taken from the Book of Genesis, the 8th chapter. It is a promise made to man that "while the earth remaineth, seedtime and harvest, hot and cold, summer and winter, day and night shall not cease."

We are told that man was placed in a garden, the garden was completed, every tree was bearing fruit, everything in the world was finished, and he was placed in the garden to dress it and to keep it. He doesn't plant it. He doesn't do a thing, but dress it and keep it. He is not called upon to make trees or to grow new trees. Everything is finished!

As we are told in John: "I have sent you to reap that whereon you bestowed no labor"- for Creation is finished. Every conceivable human drama, every little plot, every little plan in the drama of life is already worked out, as mere possibilities while we are not in them, but they are overpoweringly real when we are in them. So man can get in touch with that particular state of his choice, for my imagination can put me in touch inwardly with the state desired so I and in it. If I am in it I will realize it in my world.

The states in which we find ourselves are the seed time. The harvest is simply the encountering of events and circumstances of life. Man's memory is so short he forgets the seedtime; but all ends run true to origins. So if the origin say is misfortune, the end will be misfortune. But when you reap misfortune, you wonder: "Why should it happen to me? When have I set a thing like this in motion? Haven't I given to the poor? Haven't I attended service? Haven't I prayed daily, and why should these things happen?"

But you see, my God never forgets. Because he always gives the end in harmony with the origin. And you and I are selectors. We don't make; we are not creators. Creation is finished.

This is the whole vast world of creation as told us in Ecclesiastes: "I Am the Beginning and the End. There is nothing to come that has not been and is." So look upon creation; it is finished. And you and I are only selectors of that, which is, by selectors I mean that you and I have the privilege.

We may not exercise it, but it is our privilege to select that aspect of reality to which we will respond. And in responding to it, we bring it into existence for ourselves. Not knowing that we are so privileged, we simply go through the world reflecting the circumstances of life, not realizing we have the power to create or to project the circumstance of life. So, now, let us analyze what I personally mean by seedtime.

If everything is finished and completed, then why the promise there shall be seedtime and harvest as long as the earth remains? Now seedtime, to those who are here this morning, as we should really know, we are not taking it literally. Our seedtime is that moment of time when you and I react to anything in this world. It may be to an object; it may be to an individual; it may be to a bit of news that we have overheard. But the moment of reaction, *that* emotional response is our attitude.

Our attitudes are the seedtimes of life. And although we may not remember the seedtime or the moment of response, Nature never forgets. And when it suddenly appears in our world, that suddenness is only the emergence of a hidden continuity. It was continuous from the moment of reaction, until it appeared in the world. Its appearance in the world is the harvest.

So you and I may harvest anything we desire; but we must first have a seedtime. It must be preceded by a moment of response or an attitude. How often do you say, "I approached it in the wrong attitude" or "He is in the wrong attitude" or "You must change your attitude if you would get on in this life"? I have said it - you have said it - maybe we have said it to each other - but we know the importance of right attitude.

We know this much: that I can change my attitude if circumstances change - that's automatic. We know that if something happens suddenly in my world of which up to that moment I was not aware, I, becoming aware of a change of circumstance would automatically produce in myself a change of attitude. We all do that; morning, noon and night. But that's not important. That is a reflective life. Ninety-nine percent of the world reflects life.

Now, can I consciously - can I voluntarily - can I **deliberately** produce in myself a change of attitude - one of my own discretion - one that I myself single out, and not one that is determined by or in any way is dependent on a stimulus of a change in the object itself? Must you change before I will change my attitude towards you?

We know that if you do change, I will change my attitude towards you...but must I go through life simply reflecting these changes in the objects? Can I not deliberately determine the change prior to the change in the object? For if I can, I am moving towards complete control of my fate and becoming the master of my fate - if I can assume an active positive attitude, and not depend upon changes in the object for changes in myself.

If I can do it, I really am, if not a complete master, I am becoming more in control of the circumstances of life. But 99% of the world waits for things to happen on the outside, and *then* they reflect. That's no accomplishment at all. If we would awaken and become real selectors of the beauty of this garden that God gave us, so that we can single out that particular aspect to which we will respond, then we will do it by deliberately changing our attitude towards life itself.

There is a little fable given us to show us how it is done. If you study the fable carefully, you will see the importance of imagination. That fable is the fable of the Fox and the Grapes. You all may know of it. The fox failed to obtain the grapes, and then he persuaded himself that the grapes were sour. And by imagining the grapes to be sour, he evoked in himself a change of attitude.

He no longer felt about the grapes as he formally felt. Now that's a little fable on a negative or tragic tone. You and I take the same story, but now we put it on a positive tone. We contemplate our ambitious dream; our noble concept of life. It may seem we haven't the talents to realize it. Instead of saying what the fox did - that that thing is beyond us and therefore it is sour anyway - we can take the same technique, and wonder what it would be like, had we realized it.

What would the feeling be like were we - and we name it - if I can contemplate what the feeling would be like, were I the man or woman that I want to be, were you the person that you want to be...and rejoice in that state as though it were true? I am producing it myself that emotional response necessary for seedtime.

I may not see an immediate harvest. Maybe the thing that I am now giving expression to in the form of seedtime is an oak. It is not a little mushroom that would grow overnight. Maybe my dream would take a little longer interval of time between the actual planting and the reaping. But, if I know that all these things are consistent ("See yonder fields! The sesamum was sesamum, the corn was corn. The Silence and the Darkness knew! So is a man's fate born"), so if that moment of response is the actual planting of the seed, and if it was corn, it *must* be corn when it appears in harvest time, then I can select the nature of the things I want to encounter in my world.

I can take not just Neville as a man; I can take the request, first of my circle - my intimate circle as a family man, my wife's desires for her child, for her husband, for herself, the child's desire for itself - and move beyond my little circle as a family man into the circle of friendships, move beyond that into my acquaintances, move beyond that into total strangers, impersonal states, and so on. But if I know the Law holds good, no matter when I operate it, if I do it unconsciously or consciously, you get results regardless, and the results are in harmony with the planting, with the actual seedtime.

Now what is now our seedtime today? There are maybe 2000-odd here, so we have 2000-odd different requests, multiplied by a large number because we also have requests for others you might take today, as you sit here. And you can actually contemplate what it would be like - suppose it were true. Suppose I could turn now to a friend and rejoice with him because of his good fortune, and actually carry on a mental conversation with him from the premise that he or she has already realized the dream.

Now as I do it in my imagination, I am setting up within myself a certain changed attitude in regard to that individual. I am producing within myself a certain positive, deliberate, emotional response, and that very moment that I do it, is seedtime. I will encounter that individual tomorrow or next week or next month and he or she will bear witness of that thing I plant now.

They may be totally unaware that I planted it in this garden. I am not seeking praise. I am not seeking credit. I am seeking results. If I see the man become the embodiment of the success I know that he desires and I desire for him: that's praise enough; that's payment enough. What more payment would anyone desire other than the results? For everything is a gift.

Why should I be given more? My Father gave me the garden - the whole thing in complete and full bloom - and gave me choice: the greatest gift of all. I have complete freedom of choice of the nature of the fruit I will reap in my world…but I cannot just barge into the garden and start picking fruit. There **must** be a seedtime.

I must always bear in mind that I will reap that whereon I bestowed no labor. I don't labor to make it. I simply plant it, for in that moment of response is contained all the plans, all the energy necessary to unfold that plan into a perfect wonderful objective fact which I will then harvest by becoming aware of it as an external reality. But I don't labor to make it so; I simply must know it is so. So that is our privilege. That is our choice.

If you believe it, aren't you amazed at the kind of things that you planted - at the kind of seedtime that in our ignorance, in our sleep, we allowed to actually scatter in our world? You see, some will say, "But why does God allow it?" You cannot conceive of an infinite God that is not infinite in every respect. If I was incapable, actually incapable of assuming, say, an unlovely state, I could not be my Father's son, because my Father is infinite, and if He were actually incapable of assuming any state then He would not be God.

Everything is within me. *Everything*. You cannot conceive of something that I don't contain. The most horrible thing in the world: were it not so, I could not be infinite, and, therefore, not the son of my infinite Father. So God is infinite and gave us everything, but He gave us freedom of choice that we may become selective, discriminative, and bring forth everything that is beautiful out of that garden.

If I took the piano - the 88 keys of the piano - if I could extract from that piano's keyboard every discord, I would not have a piano keyboard. If I could strike a discord and because it frightens or disturbs me, the thing grates upon my nerves; if I could now extract the keys that produced the discord, and then keep on extracting the notes that produce the discord, I would remove the 88 keys. There would be no notes left on which I could play tomorrow's harmony. But let me leave the notes and learn the art of playing the piano, so I can from the same 88 keys bring out all the harmonies of the world.

The same thing is true of man. Instead of looking at someone and accepting as final the evidence of the senses; there is someone who brought out into his own world, say disease: he is trying to analyze it from the outside - when did I contract the bug, when did I come in close contact with someone who had the bug - and they are taking him into the laboratory with his blood to try to find it there. You will never find it there. In spite of all the wisdom of man, you will find it only in the consciousness of the individual who at a moment now long forgotten, planted the thing he is now harvesting. And you are not going to find it in any external analysis at all, because things seen were never made of things that do appear.

You are warned time and time again in all the books of the Bible, but especially in that 11th chapter of the Book of Hebrews, that "Things seen were not made of things that do appear"; but no man believes it. He *insists* on finding it in things seen. So he extracts my blood, he extracts a little piece of my skin, and he starts to make an analysis of that, and he will tell me yes, he has found it in my blood. I am not denying he has found it in my blood; but *why* is it in my blood? It is in my blood or in my body, or in my world because at some point in time I, exercising the right as a free child of God, singled out some unlovely state, relative to another.

It need not be to myself; it could be to another, wherein I rejoiced in the hurt of another; where my emotional response to the news I heard was "good" - so I set it in motion; but when it happened in my world, I did not think it was so good. Still, it was my harvest - and all these things are the harvest of things you and I have planted; for all things run true to form. Don't be surprised at the suddenness in our world - someone is ill - it is only sudden because we have forgotten, and man's memory is very, very short.

Do you know that lovely little poem by George Meredith:

Forgetful is green earth;
The Gods alone Remember everlastingly; they strike Remorselessly, and ever like for like.
By their, great memories The Gods are known.

If man could only remember these moments of seedtime, he would never be surprised when the harvest appears in his world. But because he has no memory as to that moment in time when he dropped that seed, which is simply his emotional response to something he contemplated, something he overheard, something he observed, at that moment the thing was done. He didn't have to labor to bring it to harvest.

He simply encountered it as something already full grown, so he reaps now that on which he bestowed no labor, outside of choice. He selected it by his attitude - by his reaction.

Now, am I responsible for others in my world? I certainly am! When I take my little mind, my little imagination and think because it's mine - my Father gave it to me, that I can simply misuse it, it isn't going to hurt another. I tell you: you *do* have to use more control, for the simple reason I am rooted in you, and you are rooted in everyone, and all of us are rooted in God. There is no separate individual, or detached being in my Father's Kingdom. We are one. I am completely responsible for the use or misuse of my imagination.

Do you recall seeing on TV, a dramatized version of the sinking of the Titanic? Do you recall it? Have you read the book "A Night to Remember"? Well, the book itself is by Walter Lord: but 14 years before the actual harvest - or that frightful event of the sinking of the Titanic - a man in England wrote a book. He conceived this fabulous Atlantic liner and there he built her just like the Titanic (only the Titanic was not built for another 14 years), but he in his imagination conceived the liner of 800 feet. She was triple screw; she carried 3000 passengers; she carried few lifeboats because she was unsinkable; she could make 24 knots.

And then one night, he filled her to the brim with rich and complacent people. And on a cold winter night, he sunk her on an iceberg in the Atlantic. 14 years later, the White Star Line builds a ship. She is 800 feet. She is a triple screw, she can make 24 knots, and she can carry 3000 passengers. She has not enough lifeboats for passengers, but she too, is labeled unsinkable. She is filled to capacity with the rich if not complacent, but the rich certainly, because in that day, when the dollar was one hundred cents, two hundred and fifty million dollars was the worth of her passenger list. Today it would be over one billion dollars.

All the wealth of Europe and the wealth of this country was sailing on that maiden voyage out of Southampton, five nights at sea in this wonderful glorious ship. And she went down on a cold April night on an iceberg. Now that man wrote a book either to get something off his chest because he disliked the rich and the complacent, or he thought it might sell, or he thought this is the means of bringing him a dollar as a writer. But, whatever was the motive behind his book - which by the way, he called "Futility" to show the utter futility of accumulated wealth - an identical ship was built 14 years later, and carried the same kind of passenger list...and went down in the same manner as the fictional ship.

Is there any fiction? *There is no fiction*. Tomorrow's World is today's fiction. Today's world was yesterday's fiction - the dreams of men of yesteryear. *Wouldn't it be wonderful if I could talk with someone across space and just use a wire?* And I couldn't see that one: it would be a mile away beyond the range of my voice - then maybe five miles and maybe a thousand miles - fantastic dreams - then they came true. When they came true, suppose I could do it without the means of a wire. And it came true! Suppose now I could do it not just in an audio sense, but in a video sense as well. Suppose I could be *seen*? And that came true; but when they were conceived, they were all fictional - all unreal.

There is nothing unreal, because God is infinite, and God has finished creation. You cannot conceive of something that your Father has not only done and conceived of it, but is worked out in detail, with all its ramifications. You and I are only becoming aware of increasing portions of that which already is. We are not making a thing - we are discovering God's wonderful world.

But now in this church - at least here it should be done, for this is a church of the mind: this is science of mind, where there is a science to planting and you do it in a certain scientific manner. You just don't walk the street and reflect; read the papers and reflect - you go out a more positive person than people who gather in similar areas, for the simple reason they go just to hear a service and to be told how bad the world is.

You're not coming here to be told how bad the world is. For if you believe it is bad, there is something you must do about it. Because you have planted the world. You have your seedtime. So here, people gather to be told how to operate this wonderful gift that the Father gave them.

There is this wonderful mind and imagination. So you are told to go out and be picky in your selection.

Single out that aspect of reality to which you want to respond: success, health, dignity, nobility - something wonderful that you contribute to the good of the world. As you walk by you are contributing to society. You contribute to the community in which you live, not necessarily by giving dollars; but you contribute by your wonderful seedtime.

If, in your community, you see the need of maybe a church, you see the need of some wonderful school, you don't wait until people get together. You actually, in your mind's eye, contemplate the joy that is yours because of the wonderful school here for the children; a wonderful church here to lift man spiritually, and you wonder what it would be like were it true. You feel the thrill of witnessing it within. That is seedtime. Then in a way that you do not know, and you need not labor to produce, will encounter that school and that church and these lovely things in your community.

So you plant the seed and let others, who think that they are bringing it into being, let them think so. You go about this world planting the good - that is why you are here. We are gathered here on Sunday mornings to discover more and more about this wonderful gift that God gave us, that we may single out all the lovely things in the world and bring them to birth in our world.

This morning you take not only yourself - start with self - then turn to a friend in your mind's eye, and congratulate him on his good fortune - congratulate him on his expansion in his world, and actually feel the thrill of such contact - at that moment of response that was a changed attitude in regard to that friend - at that moment you planted. Now, in a way you do not know and you need not know, that seed is going to go through its normal natural hidden passage and appear as a reality in your world.

Then you will know the power latent within you, and you will stop reflecting life, and you become one what I call a true creator in the sense that you are creating by selecting wise, wise, lovely things in this world, and giving them expression in this world of ours. So that's what I mean by seedtime and harvest; the importance of the right attitude. And you can do it. You need not wait for circumstances to change. You need not wait for the stimulus of a change in the object to produce in yourself the change of attitude.

In your office, does the boss act in a rude way towards you? Well then, what would it be like if he now saw in you the helpful person that you really are, or want to be? Suppose he saw in you someone he could praise for their work and raise up in the salary world, giving an increase in salary because of your added effort; suppose he could see that in you. Contemplate the boss seeing that in you as though he saw it and rewarded you with an increase. That moment, is the moment of planting.

It may not come tonight, it may not even come this week in your paycheck; but it will come. You simply keep on planting those lovely things. But if every day when you leave the office, you say, "What a jerk", and you go home and discuss them with your mother or your husband or your wife or someone else, and they sympathize because they really believe you, all of you are playing the same reflective, negative approach to life.

But, if as you head home, you walk in the attitude that they had done it - they had increased your income, they had praised your work - and day after day, in spite of other things to the contrary, you persist in it: do you know they will do it? You will produce in them a change of heart, because you first produced it in yourself, and they will see in you qualities that they cannot now see. And then your whole vast world begins to blossom. You do it in every sense of the word.

Do you know someone who is lonely - one who really should be happily married in this world? What would it be like if you were told, not by the individual necessarily, but by a third party of the good news concerning John, concerning Mary, or someone else - someone desiring a lovely and gracious home? What would it be like?

Don't be envious. Try to rejoice. Feel the joy that is theirs, and that moment is seedtime for them. They will harvest it - and that is our opportunity to go through the world planting (and planting wisely).

Unfortunately, too many of us in church movements - I don't think you will find it in this church - but too many of us in church movements have a very serious attitude towards life. And, of course, the basic attitude *is* the attitude towards life, not necessarily the individual attitude towards an object or towards an individual, but the attitude itself that the individual adopts through life, towards life, and they have a very serious one. Well, Orage very wisely and very humorously said the serious attitude is this: that they really believe that God has an enormous struggle against helpless odds. And he said that produces in the individual the emotion of "helping poor Father". They go to help "poor Father", who has created the world and gave it to his children.

Now he brought up another interesting point of the scientific attitude towards life. Having discovered the little molecule or the little atom and the wonderful construction, that is, theoretically - having discovered this wonderful orderly construction of the bricks that make up the world, their attitude is one of orderly insignificance because they believe the world is gradually burning itself out. So no matter how orderly it is, if they really believe the sun will eventually go out and the earth will consume all its resources.

What other attitude could they adopt, besides "all dressed up with nowhere to go"? Because if eventually it is all going to be nothing anyway, no matter how orderly it is today, it could only be orderly insignificance. But I tell you, as one who has seen beyond the veil, there is no such thing as is coming to an end. Life is forever, and forever, and forever. And forever you are moving up this everlasting pilgrimage revealing the infinite glories of your Father.

So go out wisely today. Go out determined to become more selective, and more discrete in your choice of ideas you will entertain. Single out an idea that would bless an individual, and produce in yourself the emotional response that you have witnessed that state in his world. And know, that at that moment of response, you planted for that individual, and he or she is rooted in you.

There is no such thing as "they will not be found in your world", for they are rooted in you. Everyone is rooted in you. Therefore, you will not lose them. It is planted relative to that being and that being is going to harvest it, and you will know the harvest when it appears in their world. You simply plant, and let the harvest take care of itself.

Six

The True Apostle Paul

If tonight I had a wish for you, I could not think of anything greater than to wish that you would now experience the story of Paul. I do not know if you have ever asked yourself: who *is* Paul?

Paul is not mentioned in any non-biblical work of the 1st Century, outside of the Bible; and yet, he wrote so many letters - seemingly from jail; and they have been recorded. Yet, there is no record of any Paul being in the jail. And certainly, he would be recorded. So: who *is* Paul?

Paul is that last state of consciousness that man must reach if he would experience the reality of God.

You and I have ambitions in the world. Some want to be dictators, doctors, lawyers, scientists. All these are in order. But there will come a time in the life of man when there will be a hunger sent upon him, as we are told in the Book of Amos: "It will not be a famine for bread or a thirst for water, but for the hearing of the Word of God." (Amos 8:11) And only an experience of God can satisfy this hunger. That is that state of consciousness called "Paul."

Only an experience of God can satisfy him. Not a thing in the world could satisfy him. So, if I wish this night that you would have the experience of Paul, I am wishing for you that you would have the experience of God; that that final hunger would be satisfied within you, that you would actually know the experience of the reality of God.

At the very end of the Book of Acts, when they tell the story of his end, they said that "he expounded the matter to them from morning to evening, testifying to the kingdom of God, and trying to convince them about Jesus, both from the law of Moses and from the prophets. And some believed from what they heard, while others disbelieved." (Acts 28:23 & 24) That is the story. Some believe it; others disbelieve it. You will find this in every walk of life.

Now, Paul is the one who started the movement, as it were. He found God's plan of salvation, and he called it a mystery. Paul uses the word "mystery" no less than twenty times. He tells us, "It is a mystery." He speaks of it as a pattern - a pattern of words. When he writes his Letter to Timothy, he said, "Follow the pattern of the sound words which you have heard from me. Guard the truth that has been entrusted to you by the Holy Spirit who dwells within us." (II Timothy 1:13 & 14)

He tells it in his letter to the Galatians, having spoken to the Galatians and explained the mystery of Christ. Then he says to them, "O foolish Galatians, who has bewitched you, before whose eyes Jesus Christ was publicly portrayed as crucified? Let me ask you only this: Did you receive the truth of the Spirit by works of the law, or by hearing with faith? Are you so foolish? Having begun with the Spirit, are you now ending with the flesh?" (Galatians 3:1-3)

Paul saw that the Godhead was veiled in flesh and blood, and so he could say, "When it pleased God to reveal His son *in me*, I conferred not with flesh and blood" (Galatians 1:16). The outer, rational mind could not understand revealed truth, for **revealed truth cannot be logically proven**. So, to whom would I turn and ask them to throw light on my experience if my experience is not within the framework of the rational mind?

If I tell you what I experienced and there is not a thing that you can do about it on this level, then how would I turn to you or any one in the world and ask for some light upon the experience? So, having had the experience that only an experience of God could satisfy, he couldn't go to the rational mind, which he called "flesh and blood."

Now, when he uses the word "Christ," remember the word "Christ" means "Messiah." In the Old Testament the word "Christ" is not used, but the word "Messiah" is; so "Messiah" was the Promise.

Now he said, "Henceforth I regard no one from the human point of view, even though I once regarded"; now he used the word "Christ." Now let's use the word, "Messiah": "Even though I once regarded the Messiah from a human point of view, I regard him thus no longer" (II Corinthians 5:16). Having had the experience, he was not looking for any flesh-and-blood savior called "Messiah:" He *experienced* Messiah. "When it pleased God to reveal His son in me, I conferred not with flesh and blood."

Now he said, "I have been crucified with Christ," - which means "Messiah," "nevertheless I live, yet not I, but Messiah lives in me; and the life I now live in the flesh, I live by faith in the Son of God who loved me and gave himself for me." (Galatians 1:20) Now, you put it all together, and I will try to unfold a certain pattern for you.

Jesus is the "Pattern Man". That pattern is hidden in man. And he asks the question in his Letter to the Corinthians: "Do you not realize that Jesus Christ is in you? Unless of course you have failed to meet the test" (II Corinthians 13:5). I hope you realize that **we** have not failed in meeting the test. But I'll give you a quick test:

"Jesus Christ." Now what did you, at that moment, think? Something on the outside? Let me repeat it: "Do you not realize that Jesus Christ is in you? Unless of course you have failed to meet the test." Now, "Jesus Christ"; what does the mind do? Go on the outside to some existent something external to yourself? Then you have failed to meet the test, for Jesus Christ is in you. Now, that Pattern has to unfold within you. It can't unfold within you as long as you have a concept of Jesus Christ as flesh and blood.

Even in this morning's paper, I could hardly believe my eyes. Here is a new paper from the Vatican, giving new guidelines, but insisting on the tradition that must be kept. And the tradition that they mention is that the virginity of Mary must be sustained. Well, if you read the 6th Chapter of the Book of Mark, I don't see how any one with a brain in his head could sustain that story, if you take it as secular history.

If you aren't familiar with the 6th Chapter of the Book of Mark, let me quote it for you. "Is not this the carpenter, the son of Mary and the brother of James and Joses, and Simon and Juda; and are not his sisters here with us?" (Mark 6:3)

So, they mention 6 members of his family: 4 brothers and at least 2 sisters; with himself as the 7th. And now I must look upon this as secular history and say that the mother of the brood remains the virgin! But they omit the 6 that are mentioned and say she only had one, and justify it by saying that Joseph had these others by some other woman. That is not mentioned in Scripture at all.

Now I am called upon by today's directive to admit that the Pope is infallible. Well now, that is the height of nonsense; just complete, silly nonsense. I don't care what you have had as a background in religion, that statement is stupid. Religion has not a thing - **true** religion hasn't a thing to do with secular history. It is **salvation** history. The whole thing unfolds in you. **It's all about you!** It takes place within your own wonderful skull. That's where it takes place. The Being spoken of as the Lord in the Bible is your own wonderful "I AM." That's God!

Your own wonderful human imagination - that is the Lord. One day, when you get rid of some physical "Christ" - some physical being external to yourself - you make room for the stirring of this Pattern within you; and the pattern unfolds within you. Paul said, "I refuse to admit any one but Jesus Christ, and him crucified" (I Corinthians 2:2).

You hear the word "crucified" and you think of some cruel act, don't you? It isn't. Let me share with you my experience of the crucifixion. *It is sheer bliss.*

The 42nd Chapter of Psalms - or the 42nd Psalm, if you prefer - tells a story of remembrance: "And these things I remember", (Psalms 42:4) and now he recites what he remembers: how he went with the throng and led them in procession to a house of God. It was a gay and happy crowd. That night I led them in procession to the house of God. They were altogether - I would say - thrilled beyond measure because we are leading to the house of God. A voice rang out as I led them, and the voice said, "And God walks with them."

A woman at my side -- to my right, she answered the voice; and she said, "If God walks with us, where is He?" And the voice replied, "At your side." She turned to her left, looked into my face; and then she said, "What! Is Neville God?" And the voice replied, "Yes, in the act of waking."

Then the voice said to me -- and to me only; it came from the very depths of my being: "I laid myself down within you to sleep; and as I slept, I dreamt a dream. I dreamed..." and I knew exactly what he was dreaming. He was dreaming that He is I. I also knew that when He woke from His dream, I am He. The two would cease to be two, and they would become one. He is dreaming my life until He awakes within me; but when He awakes within me, He is not another. He awakes as the being in whom He fell asleep, whose life He is dreaming. That, I did know!

And then this happened: I felt myself move quickly from this wonderful crowd moving towards the seeming House of God, and then suddenly I am "nailed" upon this body with these six vortices. My head is a vortex; my two hands are vortices; my right side is a vortex; and my two feet - the soles of my feet are vortices. And I tell you, it is *sheer ecstasy*. That's the crucifixion! That is when God crucified Himself upon this cross called "man of flesh and blood."

Well, no one can attain to bliss unless he is generated here on earth. So, you and I are here; and God deliberately laid Himself down within us to dream our lives, and He's dreaming that He is you. And one day He will awake, and He is you, and you are God! - without loss of identity. I will know you just as I know you now, but you will be raised to the Ninth degree of beauty.

I can't quite find the words to describe the majesty and the dignity and all that is wonderful concerning you; and yet, I will know you as God. I will know you as Jim, whom I know and love as a friend, and I will still know Jimmy as God! That is the destiny for everyone in this world.

So, you can forget the historical presentation of Scripture as organized churches keep it and maintain it. Paul made the statement in his famous 13th Chapter of First Corinthians, called "Hymn in Praise of Love". In this hymn, he said, "When I was a child, I thought like a child, I spoke like a child, I reasoned like a child; but when I became a man, I gave up childish ways." (I Corinthians 13:11)

When you mature spiritually, you give up these childish ways that insist on the historical presentation of Jesus and the secular history of the Bible. And that Pattern will unfold when that child becomes a man; he stops accepting the flesh-and-blood Jesus and sees him for what he is. It's a pattern that unfolds within a man as the man within unfolds. And it begins with the Resurrection.

The Crucifixion is over for all of us. Every one has been crucified with Christ on these "garments" called the "cross. The day will come - and it starts with the Resurrection - you will rise within yourself, followed instantly by your "birth from above." For no man can enter that state called the Kingdom of God unless he is born from above. So, he spent his days from morning to evening testifying to the Kingdom of God, and trying to convince them about Jesus. Then he used as his arguments the law of Moses, reading Scripture for them, and then the prophets and the Psalms, trying to show these passages paralleled his own experience.

What passage would parallel his experience "when it pleased God to reveal his Son in me"? And the preposition is "in"; it's not "to" me, as some translators give it. When it pleased God to "reveal His Son in me" (Galatians 1:16) - that's where He is revealed - suddenly within you the Son appears, and the Son is just as told you in the Scripture, the 2nd Psalm:

And I will tell of the decree of the Lord:
He said unto me, "Thou art my son,
today I have begotten thee." (Psalms 2:7)

Whose words are these? These are the words of the Psalmist, David.

So, when He reveals His Son in you, which is called "Messiah," it is David. Then you know Who-You-Are, because he is telling of the decree of the Lord. God said unto David, "Thou art my son." Well, if David now stands before you and calls you "Father," **Who are you?** Are you not God? Are you not the Lord?

Well, I prophesy for you, you will have it. You will have that experience where David stands before you and calls you "Father." Then, and then only, you will know that you are the Lord God. All these things are going to happen to every child born of woman. How do I know when?

Let me share with you an experience. I do not think the lady is here tonight; she has been coming here recently, and she wrote me a letter, wherein she said: "I did not understand your books; they were given recently to me by a lady who brought me to your meetings. I've only been coming to your meetings recently, and I will come, I think, until the end." Well, they are not here tonight, but I will tell the story. She said:

"The night before last," (and her letter is dated the 11th of June; so this is the 9th of June) *"in my dream I found myself standing on the corner waiting for a streetcar or a bus, and they came by and the crowds got on, and I let every one go by. And I wondered to myself, 'If across the way, from the apartment house, some one is seeing me standing here, they will wonder: what's wrong with that woman? She could have boarded one of these buses to take her to her destination.' And here I am, waiting. Then a woman came to me and said, 'The train you are waiting for will be here in a minute. It's a black train - a long, flat, black train, with seats on both sides facing the street.'*

I looked up, and here was a long, black train coming, with seats on both sides facing the street. I boarded it. Up front I saw a crowd around a coffin.

The coffin was covered, and they were weeping; and my attention was drawn to the coffin. Then it was diverted, because I looked to the street, and here was a young woman dead - very dead. Her right arm was eaten away up to the shoulder, and she really very dead, as she lay there. Then I noticed the feet begin to move, and this woman began to be I would say restored to life, this young woman.

Then my attention was turned now to the coffin; and out of the coffin rises a man clothed in white. "At that moment I awoke, and remained awake long enough to record it, and to impress my mind with the dream. I went back to sleep, and here I am among a huge crowd. We are all going to hear Neville; but there is a feeling in the atmosphere that Neville is about to die, and we hastened our pace because we wanted to be with him if he's about to die.

So Neville puts a robe upon him, and he lays down in a ditch; and then he crawls through a small tunnel, but it seemed so easy for him to do it. He crawled through the tunnel which led him into a cave; and when he entered the cave, he stretched himself out in the cave. And all of us struggled to follow the same pattern; so we, too, crawled through this tube; and it was a very great struggle on our part.

It was not as easy as you made it seem. It seemed so effortless when you did it. Then you rose from the cave as though you had a change of mind and you came back out the same way with the same effortlessness. As you came out, we made the same effort. Again, I wondered, 'Whoever made this, why could they not have made it easier?' And so we all came out; but not everyone could make it. Many of us did, but not all could make it."

I will tell you: all will make it, but all are not ready to make it. That was an adumbration. That was a foreshadowing of what is in store for every one in this world. This is the mystery of life through death. Unless a seed, or the grain of wheat, falls into the ground and "dies," it remains alone; but if it dies, it brings forth much.

So, God "dies" - literally dies. God became as I am, that I may be as He is. He can't pretend that He is Neville. He has to actually become me; and therefore, in becoming me, He died. He is buried in my skull. That's where

He is buried. And the day will come, I will awaken, as I have awakened in my skull and come out through that tube - that very small opening. I pushed my way out, to discover the entire drama unfolding before me.

So, I say to you, you are immortal. You know why? Because you are God! God actually became as you are, and He cannot fail! For if today it is said of Paul, he tried to convince them about Jesus, and some believed from what he said, while others disbelieved, those who disbelieved are only disbelieving for a while. They are still "children." They can't get out of their minds the historical presentation of Scripture.

They must hold on like a child to some little thing that they can put their hands upon and touch it and see a physical Jesus on the outside. The day will come, when man will be robbed of historical views of Scripture. Then the Pattern can stir within, and the Pattern will unfold itself within man. And everything said of Jesus in Scripture, he or she is going to experience in the first-person-singular, present-tense experience. Then he or she will know who Jesus is, for the whole Pattern will unfold within them.

He will tell it to the best of his ability. I thought I told it clearly in my books. Evidently to this lady I didn't, for she said, "The books were given to me, and I read them, but I did not 'get' them. Having attended a few of your lectures only recently, I now begin to understand the books, but not until I heard you speak from the platform."

Well, that was quite a shock, because I thought the books were simply written, and I still do. I couldn't quite see how she could not grasp them. But by her own confession, she could not grasp it until she heard me. So, here I am telling it from the platform and trying to tell it also in books; and some believe it, and some disbelieve it. Some will think this whole thing is simply sacrilegious, that I am trying to take from them their gods. I am trying to take from them their false gods - the god that does not exist.

I am trying to take that god from them, that the real God can begin to stir within them and unfold in them, as them. Because until the false god disappears, the real God cannot awake within you. And as long as you have a Christ Jesus of flesh and blood, you do not know Christ Jesus.

Listen to the words again: "Henceforth I regard no one from the human point of view. Even though I once regarded Christ from the human point of view, I regard him thus no longer." These are the words of Paul (II Corinthians 5:16).

"I am crucified with Christ," said he; "nevertheless I live, yet not I, Christ lives in me. And the life that I now live in the flesh I live by the faith of the Son of God who loved me and gave Himself for me." (Galatians 2:20)

Well, I am telling you, your Real Being is Jesus. That's the Lord. Your real "son" is David. That's the Messiah. But you do not know that you are the Lord, and cannot know it, until your "son" appears. The day will come, he will appear; and the minute he appears, you will know exactly who he is. There will be no uncertainty as to this relationship between you, the Father, and David, the Son. It takes the Son to reveal the Father.

Now, no church in this land that I know of is teaching this; so I have been sent to tell it to you. And you are here a small audience, but what does it matter? A small audience started on the Truth can spread to the whole vast world. I am telling you what I know from experience. I am not theorizing; I am not speculating.

You are the Lord suffering from amnesia, because you have forgotten Who-You-Are. That's how complete your gift was when you became man. And the day will come, you will awaken and remember Who-You-Are, and because you are God the Father, there must be a "son" to bear witness to your fatherhood. And that "son" is David. Then you will know Who-You-Are.

Then, one by one, we will reunite into the One Being who is God the Father, without loss of our individuality - without loss of the being that we are. I will know you in Eternity, but know you as God! Now, here we only have two lectures left; and these will be in order, even though they seem repetitious. They cannot be repeated too often.

Man so quickly forgets! You go away for a month, and those you thought really understood you, when you return, they try to tell you: "I just found the most wonderful book on diets," or the most wonderful book on how to get into Heaven in another way. A friend of mine - I thought he understood it - I thought he did, for he made extravagant claims, and in the last month he sent me books by men that I knew before they died here.

We mustn't judge from appearances, I know; but as I told him over the phone when I sent the books back, "I had the dubious pleasure of knowing these men. The book that you just sent me...that man is incapable of writing a decent sentence. I knew him when he sold stocks that did not exist, and there is no transforming power in death. He is still selling stocks that do not exist! And you ask me to read this book? I wouldn't trust him as far as I could throw him."

I am not a strong man today, and he weighed - when he died - over two hundred pounds; so you can see how far I would trust him. And I thought that man really understood what I'm talking about. I'd believed that he did. That's how deceived you can be when you think that they understand you and they go away for a short while - maybe a year, and then they completely forget the message. You could tell them over and over that your own wonderful human imagination is God, and there is no other God, and don't start looking for another God; and that God is forever. His name is "I AM" forever and forever, and you can't leave it alone. That's the Lord. But He's a father, and I tell you from experience: His Son is David.

I thought he understood it, because he told me one day that he had an experience. Well, I know it was an adumbration; it was a foreshadowing. He is a very powerful thinker; so he could conjure and give himself a grand hallucination, and thought that was it. It wasn't it. That was a hallucination, when he thought - because it doesn't come that way. The dove does not come the way that he told me it came to him. It doesn't come that way.

The whole heavens becomes translucent when he comes, and the dove floats just as though it is floating on water, but it's translucent. The action of the dove is without effort; therefore it must be floating. Then it descends gently upon you; and then you, like Noah, you stretch out your hand for it, and the dove lights upon your hand just as you are told in the Book of Genesis, and you bring the dove to you. Then the dove smothers you with kisses.

But the other is a wonderful adumbration. It's a wonderful forecasting. But then, I thought that would be encouraging to him to have the adumbration to sustain him until the reality takes place. Evidently not. That is why I have to repeat it over and over and over once more, that you won't forget it.

So, when he wrote his last letter to Timothy - but Timothy was then a man of God - he was no longer a child, for he is called a "man of God." Only two are called "men of God" in Scripture: one is Moses, and one is Timothy. And so he speaks to the "man of God," but he still has to remind him to "follow the pattern of the sound words which you have heard from me. Guard the truth that has been entrusted to you by the Holy Spirit who dwells within us."

Guard it! Don't let anything come in and take from you that truth, for there is only one true way to God - only one living and true way to the Father, and it's that Pattern. The Pattern unfolds within you. That Pattern is called in Scripture "Jesus Christ," or "the Lord and His Christ." That is what it is called. And when it unfolds within you, you are the Lord, and you have a Messiah. He stands before you, and he is David.

Now, I could close my eyes this very moment in confidence that every one is going to experience this. I only hope you will not be diverted in the interval. I hope that you will actually believe what I have told you, but I know you are going to have it; and it's not anything that you saw in this morning's paper if you read what I read.

> "I am Mary," - and you can say that too:
> I am Mary, and birth to God must give,
> If I in blessedness for now and ever more would live.

There *is* no other "Mary"! That holy womb is my own skull - that's the cave that the lady saw - and you go into that cave deliberately - voluntarily, may I tell you? And you die in your dream that you are other than Who-You-Are, because you are God dreaming that you are John, that you are Neville, that you are Sasha, that you are Jan. You are dreaming these; and when your dream is over, *you* are. You have individualized yourself as Jimmy, as Sasha - everyone in the world. And only God, then, awakes; and when God awakes, we are individualized, and we are God!

So, the true Temple of God is the individuality of man, made perfect by the Holy Spirit within us. He comes within us, and we are made perfect. We, then - the individualized man - is the true temple of God! So, I will meet you - yes, you - in Eternity; and you will know me.

A lady is here tonight who wrote me a letter this past week. She said: *"Neville, I was sitting in my living room. My husband had a toothache, and he retired. I thought, Well, I would just sit and meditate. I was meditating in my living room, and suddenly I felt the Presence of God! I looked up, and there in my dining room there you were; and I knew you were Neville, but I also knew you were God! There was no uncertainty in my mind. I am looking at you. This is the Neville that I know, yet I know you are God!' And you were clothed in light - golden light, and then I must tell you,"* she said at the very end, *"You were altogether beautiful."*

Well, thank you, my dear. I do know that when you see the Being that you really are, no human words can describe that beauty. No human words can describe the majesty that is yours, the strength that is yours, the character that is yours; and through these mortal eyes you can look into any mirror, and you could never think that Eternity is long enough to bring you to that state. And yet, when it takes place, instantaneously you are that Being.

So, she saw it, as many have seen it and many will see it until I depart this world. And then many will see it after I depart this world, for I know what I'm talking about. The whole story as told in the Scripture unfolded itself in me, and I am relating my own experience. I am not speculating; I am not theorizing. I am telling you exactly what happened to me.

And if this lady witnessed what I've told you that I am, all well and good. You are told in Scripture that he appeared first to Peter. Well, I did. She isn't called "Peter" here. Then to the twelve - I did. Then to five hundred. I have not heard from five hundred, but I am hearing from them. Then to James, then to the Apostles, and last "as to one untimely born" he appeared also to Paul.

Well, that is the last stage, when that one comes. Eventually it is going to unfold in him. But in her case who sits here tonight, she has qualified for the highest office, for you are told in the 9th Chapter of 1st Corinthians, when they questioned him concerning his apostleship he said, "Am I not free? Am I not an Apostle? Have I not seen the Lord Jesus?"

He placed it as an indispensable prerequisite for Apostleship, to have seen the Risen Lord, for he confessed that he never saw any Jesus "after the flesh." He never saw any Jesus after the flesh - nor did he ever, he said. "Henceforth, I regard no one from the human point of view. Even though I once regarded Christ from the human point of view, I regard him thus no longer." So he saw him, but not "after the flesh."

Well, this thing talking to you here is simply a veil. The God-head is veiled in flesh and blood, and you see the flesh. The lady saw that which is veiled. And that's what I am talking about. Your present "garment" veils the Being that you are; and the Being that you really are is God! And there is nothing but God. But while we "wear" it and still are "children".

Well then: as a child, I think as a child, and I reason as a child, and I talk as a child; but when we become men, we give up childish ways. So we can actually think abstractly, and not have to take this wonderful Pattern and clothe it in flesh in order to understand it. So, when he speaks of the mystery, he said, "Christ in you is the mystery of which I speak. That is the hope of glory."

"I tell you a mystery," he said.

And **twenty times** he uses the word "mystery". And the churches speak of Paul's martyrdom. The Bible, you can scour the Bible from beginning to end, and you will not find one word in Scripture concerning any martyrdom of Paul. Yet the churches teach that he was martyred, that maybe he was fed to the lions by Nero. It hasn't a thing to do with that.

The word "martyr" and the word "witness" are one and the same in Scripture. So, he is a witness to the truth. But now, because the word "witness" was translated as "martyr," they say he was a martyr. The word is "martyr," but the translation - the meaning of the word - is "witness." He said, "I have come to bear witness to the truth," when he stands before the judge and declares that his kingdom is not of this world. "For this I was born. For this I have come into the world." For what purpose? To bear witness to the truth. That word translated as "witness" is the same word as "martyr."

"I have come to bear witness to the truth"; and they claim he was murdered? No!

I tell you what I have told you earlier tonight: I have experienced crucifixion, as Paul said he did. And it is ecstasy; *sheer* ecstasy! Six vortices - whirling vortices: a vortex, a vortex, a vortex, a vortex, and then the two feet are vortices; and I can't tell you the thrill when you are drawn into this body through these six vortices! And then the voice rings out: *"I laid myself down within you to sleep; and as I slept, I dreamt a dream. I dreamt..."*

Yes, I knew exactly what he is dreaming. He is dreaming that He is I; and when He awakens, I am He! "The two shall become one." For here was His emanation, yet His "wife, till the sleep of Death is past." And when that sleep of death is over and He awakes, He awakes in me as the Being in whom He fell asleep, and I am He! Because He was a father when He laid Himself down within me, when He wakes He is still a father; therefore, I am a father. So, He became me; and therefore that Son that was His Son is now my "son". And His Son is David, and David calls me "Father." <u>That</u> is the mystery.

You dwell upon it. You will be tempted to go astray and follow after strange gods. But stick to it. I have told you what I know; and so, if you are tempted, come back to it. As often as you are led astray, come back to it. Try to remember what I have told you. But don't turn away. I plead with you because I am telling you what is in store for you: ***Joy beyond measure.*** For we are all destined to enter that Kingdom called the Kingdom of God.

Seven

The Identical Harvest

In the very beginning, God established the Law of the Identical Harvest. "And God said, Let the earth put forth vegetation: Plants bearing seed and fruit trees bearing fruit in which is their seed, each according to its kind; and it was so." (Genesis 1:24) Now we are warned: "Do not be deceived, for God is not mocked. As a man sows, so shall he reap." (Galatians 6:7)

So, do not try for one moment to deceive yourself. All that is taking place in your world, you planted. There is only one Planter in the world, and the Planter is God; but man looks for God outside of himself; and we are warned that He is within us. We are told to examine ourselves. "Test yourselves. Do you not realize that Jesus Christ is in you? Unless, of course, you fail to meet the test." (II Corinthians 13:5, Rev. Standard Ver) So, within us is the Lord Jesus Christ! And we are told: "By him all things were made, and without Him was not anything made that was made." (John 1:3)

Now, where is He? Who is He? If He is in me, and He is the cause of the phenomena of my life and everyone's life, then where is He? I should find Him. It's the most important search in the world - and I have found Him! Christ-in-you is your own wonderful human imagination. <u>That</u> is the Lord! Your every imagined act plants a seed, and the harvest is nothing more than the multiplication of that same seed. You **cannot** change it.

How do I plant the seed? Well, I could plant it unwittingly, as most of us do. I read the morning's paper, and I react emotionally. At that moment,

I planted a seed! You tell me a story, and I react emotionally. At that very moment I planted a seed; and, I am going to reap it, with an identical harvest.

Most of us don't remember. We don't remember the moment when we planted the seed; but every natural effect has a spiritual cause. A "natural" cause only seems; it is a delusion of a withering vegetable memory. We cannot quite relate the harvest to anything that we've done. Let me now tell you a simple little story.

In March, the Los Angeles Times printed a brief story about a lost church organ. The minister called in the detectives and announced that the church organ was stolen. He gave a description of the organ, to the best of his ability. They found what they thought to be the organ that was lost, but all identification marks were removed.

The serial number, and any other identifiers, had been removed. The minister said to the detectives, "Look into the back of the organ and see if you find a paperclip with a little piece of paper and a number clipped to it." The detective asked "Why?" and the minister said, "I placed it there." He asked again, "Why?" The minister said, "Just in case."

Now, he is preaching the story of Christ. "Just in case..." That is when he planted loss - with the "just in case." To tell him that he was the source of the loss of that organ, he would strike you if he was bigger. Really, he was the cause of that loss; but you couldn't tell him that. Yet he will repeat from the pulpit: "Be not deceived, for God is not mocked." He will even quote Job: "My fears have come upon me." (Job 4:14) For my preconceived acts, whether they be in love or in fear, they are seeds, and I **must** reap them.

I will share one that is very personal. *When* I planted it, I do not know, but I *had* to have planted it. And I will show you that, even though you plant unlovely things unawares, you need not be the victim. You can revise it, and change it, even though you are confronted with a seemingly insoluble problem.

When I left here last July, I checked two suitcases at the airport. When I arrived in Los Angeles, one was missing. The contents I could not replace for $1500. They were all the lovely dresses that my wife has, and all her dresses are made by a certain couturier in Beverly Hills, and not one is under $195. She'd made these dresses over the years for her. They were not new, but I couldn't replace any one of them for less than $195 - plus other things in that suitcase. My suits were in another suitcase, perfectly all right. I recorded the loss. They said, "When we find it, if we find it, we will send it right over to you, Mr. Goddard."

After five days and not a word, we called; and they said, "It is lost. We've made every effort, and it cannot be found. Put in a claim and send it off to San Diego, the headquarters for the PSA office." My wife did the legitimate thing in the world of Caesar. She itemized the contents to the best of her ability, and what it would take to replace the items in that suitcase.

About 2 o'clock that morning I awoke and said, "Now, look here. I teach this principle; and, so, I have brought about a loss in my own world. I will have none of it! I teach Revision. I heard what the man said over the telephone: 'The thing is lost. They cannot find it; we have looked high and low.'"

Then you read in the papers that hundreds of millions of dollars are stolen every year at our airports, depots, and the wharves across the country; and it's an inside job, as it were. So, at 2 o'clock in the morning, I took up my suitcase. I felt the weight of it; I could *feel* the weight. I could see in my mind's eye the gray bag with the black leather. I could actually *feel* it, and I felt it with a sense of relief, for of all the pleasures in the world, relief is the most keenly felt.

When you are expecting someone, and they are late - someone you truly love, and it gets later and later and you get anxious, and then you hear a familiar voice; you know the relief that comes? Well, now, that's what you do when you feel that relief. And, then, I dropped it and got up and went into my living room, and simply read my Bible.

It was early. We have a lovely apartment, and it was quiet. We have no neighbors. I turned on the lights and read my Bible. The next day: no report. The following day, I received a letter postmarked San Francisco, with a strange, peculiar printing of my name: Neville Goddard. The address was correct. When I opened the letter, there was a little note in the same peculiar printing that read: "Your suitcase is in Box 524. Sorry. The Phantom"; and a key was enclosed. So, I called the security guards at the Los Angeles airport, and told them the contents of the letter. I said, "I have the key."

One of them called back within 10 minutes to tell me that there was no such box in Los Angeles. I reminded him that the letter came from San Francisco; so he said, "All right, I'll call you back. " He called San Francisco, and the security guards got the local police, and they opened 524, and there was my suitcase. They opened it up in the presence of the policemen, and the whole thing was completely ransacked; utterly turned inside out. They sealed it, flew it down, and asked me to come over with my wife; and in our presence, the L.A. security guards opened that suitcase.

Not a handkerchief was missing! Everything was turned inside out. The man was most apologetic, and said, "Mr. Goddard, I am awfully sorry. We are sorry for the Company. These things happen. We do not know how they happen, but they happen. May we clean the things for you?" I said, "No; that is something that my wife and I do every year. We travel for more than 2 weeks. Everything we wear is dry-cleaned. So, it is a little problem of ours, and we've always done it."

Then he gave me his personal card and said, "The next time you and Mrs. Goddard travel on PSA, you are our guests." I took the card and gave it to my wife; and now we are here and going back as the guests of PSA. But we did not lose one handkerchief - not a thing; but it *was* a complete mess. What they were looking for, I do not know; but they found nothing there. However, that's done.

Here is a story about my good friend Freedom Barry. About 3 months ago, Freedom called me. He was distressed, and in a panic. He said:

"Neville, my most precious possession is my grand piano. I can't replace it for $4,000. It's only insured for two. Well, it needed certain repairs; so I sent it back to the factory for the repairs. When it was done, they called me and said they would not deliver it until I came to the factory and tried it and saw the work done, and then agreed to the work. It was a $400 job."

So, he made the trip to the factory, tested the piano, and approved it. They said they would send it off, and the date given for delivery was a Tuesday. He remained in all day on Tuesday; but no piano. He remained in on Wednesday; and no piano. On Thursday he called, and they said, "We were waiting for a full load. That's why we didn't get it off on time; but it is off now. But, unfortunately, we can't find the truck or the driver. They have both disappeared."

At that point Freedom panicked. He said, "You know, I am so close to the picture, I can't do a thing. Were it another person, I could do it. But I can't do it for myself, and the one person in this world I can turn to in confidence happens to be you. Will you help me bring back my piano?"

I thanked him for the confidence he had in me; and then, as I hung up the telephone, I went into my bedroom, and proceeded to put myself into the mood of hearing his voice - as I had just heard it - telling me that he has the piano. That night, a lovely piano concerto was on. Every night, between 8 and 10, our local station KFAC plays 2-3 hours of lovely classical music.

This night in particular they were playing beautiful piano concertos. So, I imagined it was Freedom. I sat there entranced with the beauty of the music, and I assumed it was Freedom playing; and then I turned it off just as it came to the end, so I would not hear who played it. I assumed it was Freedom. Then, in my imagination, I put my hands upon his shoulders and thanked him for the joy that he gave me, and felt completely relieved in what I had done.

Two days later, he phoned to say they had found the man. At first he would not reveal what he had done with the truck or its contents, but eventually he confessed, and they got the piano. So the piano is back in Freedom's house. All it needed was a tuning due to the long ride, and the extreme heat through the day; and the cold at night. Now he has his lovely piano, and he treasures that piano more today than he did prior to the loss of it. It's like a lost son coming home.

So, here we have a law. It's a principle; and morning, noon and night, you and I are operating this principle; and we **can't** stop it. If the world seems confused today, it's confused because we, the operant power, made it what it is. There is no power outside of man doing anything. Why? Because God became man, that man may become God! He actually became as I am, that I may be as He is! He's not pretending that He's Neville; He actually *became* Neville. He's not pretending that He is you; He actually *became* you.

And in you, He is your own *wonderful* human imagination; and one day you will know it. You will know it beyond all worldly doubts. When He completely awakens within you, and His Son calls you Father: then you will know it. But until His Son calls you Father, and you know that relationship...try it. Test yourself to see whether you are holding to the faith. What faith? People say, "the Christian faith." Well, what is the Christian faith? "I believe in the Lord Jesus Christ." Well, do you believe that He is in you? "No." Well, then, you don't believe in the Lord Jesus Christ! Do you not realize that the Lord Jesus Christ is in you, and that there is no other lord?

So, as Blake said:

"Babel mocks, saying there is no God or Son of God; That Thou, O Human Imagination, O Divine Body of the Lord Jesus Christ art all a delusion; but I know Thee, O Lord, when Thou arisest upon my weary eyes, even in this dungeon and this iron mill; for Thou also sufferest with me, although I behold Thee not. And the Divine Voice answers: "Fear not! Lo, I am with you always. Only believe in me, that I have power to raise from death Thy Brother who sleepeth in Albion." (From "Jerusalem")

That, I know from experience. He can raise from death the One who sleeps in Universal Man, called Albion. One day you will experience it. You will actually experience the story of the Lord Jesus Christ! And when you experience it, you <u>are</u> the Lord Jesus Christ! You'll experience it in a first-person, singular, present-tense experience; and His Son calls you Father.

You say, "What! Jesus has a son?! He *is* a son", the world will say. The world does not understand the mystery of the Lord Jesus Christ. He *is* the Father. "Have I been so long with you, and yet you do not know me, Philip? He who has seen me has seen the Father. How, then, can you call me and ask me to tell you about the Father? I've been so long with you, and yet you do not know me." "I and the Father are one." (John 10:30)

And then you will say, "But did he not also say, 'The Father is greater than I?'" Yes; but the Lord is not inferior as to His Essential Being; only as to the <u>office</u>, as the one that He sent. But he tells us the Sender and the Sent are one. So, when you see me, you see Him who sent me; but in the office of the Sent, I am inferior as to my Essential Being - the Sender who sent me.

And, so, he said his law holds good forever. Well, what is his law? Whatever you desire, *believe* that you have received it, *and you will*. **That's the law.** Whoever believes that what he says will come to pass, it shall be done for him.

Can you believe that? Can you *actually* believe that you can put your hand upon a friend, and tell that friend you've never seen them look better? Or hear them say they've never felt better? Can you put your hand in theirs and congratulate them on their good fortune, and have them tell you they've never had more?

Here is a simple story. A lady called me about eight months ago, all excited. She said, "Neville, will you hear for me that I have ten million dollars? I will give you one million if you will hear for me that I have ten million. Well, I have known this lady over the years. In fact, I gave her away to her husband. She had no father, and she'd asked, "Will you give me away?" I said, "Willingly; gladly."

During the reception, a lady came up to me and said, "Now, tell me, who are you?" I said, "I'm the bride's father." She said, "I paid for the service, but I saw you give her away. But, tell me now, who are you *really*?" I said, "I am the bride's father."

"Well," she said, "it so happens that I am the bride's sister!" What could you do? She *was* the bride's sister. But I did not know she had a sister.

However, she called and asked me to hear she had ten million dollars. About two months later she called. She could hardly speak over the excitement. She said, "You know, my brother received from this lady - a very, very elderly lady - the entire estate; and the estate is in excess of one hundred million dollars."

Well, I didn't ask her to hold her breath until an estate of that size was settled. The chances are she'll be gone, and others will follow her. With such an enormous estate, you will find all sorts of people claiming they are the mother, or her brother, or this, that, and the other. So, I didn't say one word to in any way disillusion her. She was in the mood - a mood of enormous wealth; and she walked in that state, waiting for the brother to have the estate settled. Undoubtedly he promised her ten million of the hundred million, for he knew the value of the estate. But forget that part of it: *she was in the **mood** of wealth.*

She called me one month ago, and this is her story; and this is, now, factual. She did not have to wait for this estate. She said, "You know, these two elderly ladies came into the meeting." Her husband has a little church - not much bigger than this room; and these two elderly ladies in pants, whom you wouldn't think could even contribute a dime to support that little church, said to her one day: " Do you have a mortgage on this place?" She confessed, "Yes, we have a mortgage." "How much?" She told them, and they said, "All right; we will take care of it."

They paid off the mortgage on the house and the church one hundred percent, bought her a new car, gave her the pink slip, and set up a trust fund for one thousand dollars a month for the rest of her earthly days. You see, she was **in the mood**. She was in the mood of fantastic wealth. Whether that enormous estate is ever settled or not, or whether it is true or not, at least she was in the state that called in her, by that imaginal act, **the same** identical harvest.

If you would *really* believe in the Lord Jesus Christ, and pinpoint Him as your own wonderful human imagination... there is no other lord. He literally became as you are, that you may be as He is! The Incarnation took place at Calvary, not at Bethlehem. When God became man, that's Calvary. That is the Incarnation, and He is not pretending. He had to completely empty Himself of all wisdom and all knowledge, and all power to become us! At Bethlehem, we become as He is. That's the mystery.

And here tonight, if you know who He is, and you trust Him one hundred percent, you can turn to Him, for "All things are possible to God," - all things. There is no restriction placed upon the power of God, if you know who He is. But if you have some little reservation, you will do this: "- BUT!" Well then... don't call. If you say, "Well, I will ask 3 or 4 people, in case one fails"... you don't know Christ.

If Freedom had called me and then, as he hung up, called a 2nd, a 3rd, or a 4th person, he would have no confidence in my teaching; none whatsoever. But I know Freedom, or I would never have told him to come here and teach. But I felt in Freedom the man I wanted him to be. And Freedom came here, and he taught, and he is a wonderful teacher. He doesn't teach the Promise, because he hasn't had the Promise. He's had the Law, and he knows the Law. Well, when you are so very close to it, you find it difficult to operate.

Look at your hand. If the back of your hand began to itch, it can't reach itself; but what's wrong with using your other hand to scratch? Can't this come to its assistance and scratch it? There's only one body. We are told: "There is only one body, one spirit, one Lord...one God and Father of all." (Ephesians 4:4-6)

So, as one Body, he turns to an aspect of himself, which is the one body; and he turned to the aspect of his Body in whom he had confidence, and he called me. Well, at that moment I heard him, and then dropped it. You don't do it day after day; you simply do it, and it's done! There's always an interval of time between a seed that is planted and the harvesting of that seed; so just drop it. You don't pick it up every day to see if it's really growing. You leave it, and the thing germinates, and then it comes into fruition in its own due time.

Unfortunately, we are not aware of the moment of the planting of the seed; and when the harvest appears, we deny our own harvest. We can't believe for one moment that we did it. Recently I read an interview with Mrs. Martin Luther King, the widow of the great evangelist, and she said the day that the late President Kennedy was assassinated, "My husband turned to me and said, 'That is the way I am going to die. I, too, will be assassinated.'" He was a powerfully emotional being; he identified himself with that martyrdom. Whether he wanted to be a martyr for his own cause or not, I do not know. But her own words: "My husband said to me when he heard of the story of the assassination of Kennedy, 'That's the way I am going to be killed. I am going out just like that.'"

Now, you tell that man that he did it, and the one who now serves 99 years was only the means by which his will was externalized, he would not believe it. There's always somebody ready, waiting to aid the externalization of my will; and my will is a simple imaginal act, that's all. And, then you, if you can be used - if you are not in that state that you can be used, you will not be used against your will. But there are those who are falling into all kinds of states in this world.

There are those who feel at home being a thief! Well, if I feel that I have lost something, the states occupied by men who believe themselves to be thieves - they will fulfill my will for me. If I feel that I am secure, there are those in the world who will play their part and aid the birth of my feeling that I am secure. It's entirely up to us. **What are we doing?**

Well, you cannot change this eternal Law of the Identical Harvest. You will find it in the very first chapter of the Book of Genesis. The first chapter, 11th verse states: "And God said, Let the earth put forth vegetation, plants bearing seed, and fruit trees bearing fruit in which is their seed, each according to its kind. And so it was." And not a thing has happened in the world to change that. It's the same wonderful law.

So, whatever we are today, we are by reason of the fact that we are the Sower. People love to sow. But the comforting thing is this: that the Word of God has been sown, and no one can change it. And where is it sown? It's sown in **you**.

The Word cannot return void, but must accomplish that which He purposed. For, in every child born of woman the Word of God has been planted, and that Word, in the fullness of time, will erupt; and the story of God will unfold in the man in whom He has planted it. Then that man will know he is the Lord Jesus Christ. That's the most glorious thing in the world! If you suffer now because of your strange planting, all well and good; but bear in mind: the Word of God has been planted, and you cannot fail.

Not one child born of woman in this world can fail to one day realize that they are God the Father. If one failed, the whole thing would fail. Not one can fail. No, not even a Hitler - not even a Stalin; for behind the mask called Stalin, and the mask called Hitler, there is that Word of God that is perfect; and it will grow.

And, one day, it will erupt. They have gone from this world only to our physical senses, but they haven't really gone. They are in a world just like this, terrestrial, in a body that is new - unaccountably new, but a <u>new</u> body, in an environment best suited for the work yet to be done in them, for: "He who began a good work in you will bring it to completion at the revelation of Jesus Christ." So, the whole thing is the process of the unfolding of the Word in man. The day will come, and it comes with shocking suddenness.

We are told: "You must be born from above; for unless you are born from above, you cannot enter the Kingdom of Heaven, which means the New Age. But while you are here in *this* age, if you are not "born from above" before the so-called "death" takes place, "death" is only the passing through a door; but you do not die. **Nothing** dies!

You pass through the door. Those who remain cannot see you beyond the door, but you aren't dead; you are just as alive as you are here: in a body like this, only it's young; not a babe, but about 20 years of age, in an environment best suited for the work that you must still do. And, then, one day you are "born from above"; and from then on, you enter an entirely different world: a New Age.

It's not an area; it's a body. And wherever you are, clothed in that body, everything is perfect. Nothing can remain imperfect in your presence, wherever you are! So, the Kingdom of Heaven is not an area. It's not a realm. It is a body! Wherever you are, nothing remains dead. Everything is made alive and perfect. Trees that are long dead and turned to stone burst into flower as you walk by. Things that are completely wrong are perfect as you walk by. Seeds that are not growing spring and rise when you go by. It is a living body.

Yes, the Kingdom of Heaven is a body! It's the Perfect Body. It is the body of the Risen Lord within you, which is the Lord Jesus Christ. So, nothing can remain imperfect when you are "born from above." But tonight, in the practical world in which we live here, which will still be with you when you go through the gate called "death" (it will be the practical world), you will find this principle still operating. Everyone who is not "born from above" will still be looking for this principle to find out how to make things come into their world that they want. It is a simple, simple principle.

You start knowing that your own wonderful human imagination is God. That's the Lord Jesus Christ. Though I do not now know from actual experience, I will believe it, and then put Him to the test. I will test Him; and then you take a goal in life for yourself or for a friend; and then persuade yourself that things are as you would like them to be.

When you are self-persuaded that they are, you do nothing. The whole vast world will aid in the birth of that assumption. All you need do is **assume that things are as you want them to be**, and in that state let it go; and all things will move to aid the birth of your assumption. There's no need to go to any one.

First of all, the whole wide world is simply yourself externalized anyway. There's no need to "get even" when an injustice is done to you. Just "go about your Father's business", forget it, and continue doing good. You won't grow weary in the doing of good, for in due season you will reap, *if* you do not grow weary.

So, even when you feel you were wronged: forget it. If I had placed my mind on the one who did it, or who I thought did it, I would still be looking for my wife's suitcase. But I completely forgot that; and when Caesar called, I turned to the Only One Who Never Fails; and that One, and one's own imagination, are one and the same.

You see, we **exist** in physical bodies, but we **live** in imagination. You can't get away from it. That is your immortal body. So, you live in imagination; you only exist in physical bodies. And these bodies will turn to dust, but will be restored quickly - instantaneously even! The world will say, "How do you know?"

Well, I know. I know from experience; I'm not speculating. I see my friends - those who have gone - and they are in a world just like this. I meet them. They were not "born from above" while they were here; and they are not yet "born from above" now that they are there. And so, I meet them, and I discuss with them and teach them this principle. But I cannot go beyond this, for then I will not be functioning in that sphere.

Having gone through the four dramatic scenes, as discussed in Scripture, I've reached the end of the drama. But only now, while I am still anchored to this body, can I meet them at night when I put this thing we call the physical body down, and go to sleep. I meet my father, my mother, my brothers; and I instruct them concerning this principle. Then they are instructing themselves; and I hope here in the world you, too, will become teachers and teach, even as the body sleeps on the bed.

After all: what else should one learn? If you know there is a principle by which you can be what you want to be in this world, then what else is important? And you simply lead a nice, wonderful, free life, hurting no one, and just simply doing what you consider the good as you understand it...when you take it to heart and do not turn back.

Test yourself everyday to see whether you are holding to the faith - and the faith is not believing in the Protestant faith, or the Catholic faith, or the Lutheran faith, or the Jewish faith. No, the faith is simply: "Do you believe in God?" For God is in you. His name is in you, and He and His name are one, and His name is: "I AM." That's God.

So if you say, "I am Mary", all right; now you have put something on it. If you say, "I am Larry", you've put something on it. His name is "I AM". Well, you can put: "I am wealthy"; "I am secure"; "I am wanted"; "I am happy." You can put these attributes on it, and walk in the state of consciousness that you are actually this living state that says "I am happy"...and in a way that you do not even know, you'll be happy. You will be happy here while you seemingly are awake, and you will be happy there while you seemingly are asleep.

The day that you *really* awake - what a shock it will be! Because if you tell the whole world that they are sound asleep, they won't believe it. If I told the world tonight, "You are sound, sound asleep, and the Dreamer in you is dreaming the dream, and the Dreamer is God," they would think I'm insane. Before the day it happened to me, I would have told anyone who told me that, that they were insane too.

And when I, the Dreamer, awoke within my own skull, I wondered: who put me here? How long have I been here? And here, all along, I had been dreaming, and the dream seemed so objectively real, that I didn't realize it was all a dream - or that I myself was the dreamer of it all - or that the whole world is simply playing the part they must play - because of the nature of the dream that I was dreaming. Then I woke within myself to find who the Dreamer was. And the Dreamer was the Lord Jesus Christ!

We are told in Scripture to "leave everything and cleave to your wife until you become one"; and man thinks it means the woman you marry. **No.** THIS is my emanation. THIS is "my wife." I must cleave to it until finally the Dreamer, and the thing it's dreaming, become one. But the Dreamer is the Lord Jesus Christ.

So, wherever there are two, you are one; and you can share what you've done as experience with others, but you don't go around talking about it, because if any one ever says to you: "Look, here He is", or "Look, there He is", don't believe it; you will never really know Jesus Christ until He looks just like you. When you see Him, **He is just like you.**

We are told, He is the Rock. "But of the Rock who begot you, you are unmindful and forgot the God who gave you birth." (Deuteronomy 32:18) And they ran from the supernatural rock, and the rock was Christ. I tell you, that if the Rock of Christ is in you - and I know that it is - then the Rock is in you. And one day you will see that within that Rock there is a man; and when you see it, you will say: "Why, it is I!" You will actually see Him, and you will say, "It is I!"

The Rock became fragmented, and that Rock drew together all its different fragments and formed itself into the Human Form. And one day you will see it. It's a human form that is seated before you. As you look at it, it glows; it is alive, but with a face whose beauty you've never seen before. You have never seen such strength of character, or such majesty. Whatever you might name, that face has it in perfection. That is your face! It is you! The whole thing glows like the sun, and then explodes. That's the Man-in-you. And that Man is the Lord Jesus Christ.

We are told in Scripture, if any man should say to you: "Lo, here is Christ", or "Lo, there he is", don't believe him. Why? Because when He appears, we will know Him. Why? Because He will be like you - *just* like you; your face, beautiful as it is, raised to the ninth degree of perfection, with no blemish, and bursting with character! You've never seen such strength of character as you will see on the face that is yours. You've never seen such majesty as you will see on the face that is yours, or such beauty as on that face that will be your face.

So, the Rock as told in the 32nd chapter of Deuteronomy, is literally true. Sitting one day in the silence, contemplating nothing in particular, suddenly a rock of lovely quartz came before me. I simply looked at it, not expecting anything; and suddenly it became fragmented - broken into many pieces. Then, like a magnet, all the pieces drew together into a man seated in the lotus posture.

I looked at him; and suddenly I was looking at myself. At that moment I realized it was alive, and something I could not in eternity ever hope to be. The beauty, the majesty; and I was looking at myself! And then it began to glow. It glows ever brighter like the sun; and then it explodes, and you see the rock.

It calls to mind a lovely poem by Robert Graves:

Hold fast with both hands
To that One Love which alone,
As you search the earth, restores
Fragmentation into True Being.

"That One Love which alone restores fragmentation into True Being." Yes, that Rock *was* fragmented; and every part of the world is your fragmented self; and when you reach the end, you will bring it all back into the One Being that became fragmented. And it is your being: the Only Being.

Glossary of Cited Verses

(In chronological order)

John 14:1-3
John 14:2,3
Genesis 25
Habakkuk 2:3
Matthew 11:11
II Corinthians 13:5
Exodus 6:3
1 John 4:19
Genesis 1:3
Luke 13
Corinthians 1:18
I Corinthians 2:6,7
I Corinthians 2:11
Acts 2:28
Matthew 1:2
Luke 1:18-23
Psalms 89
Isaiah 53
Luke 9:62
John 1:1-3
John 1:17
John 3
Hebrews 4:2
Psalms 1
Romans 17:4
Deuteronomy 30:15

Corinthians 13:14
1 Peter 1:10
Romans 8:28-30
Jeremiah 23
Mark 10:26-27
Hebrews 11
Amos 8:11
Acts 28:23-24
II Timothy 1:13-14
Galatians 3:1-3
Galatians 1:16
II Corinthians 5:16
Galatians 1:20
II Corinthians 13:5
Mark 6:3
I Corinthians 2:2
Psalms 42:4
I Corinthians 13:11
Galatians 1:16
Psalms 2:7
II Corinthians 5:16
Galatians 2:20
I Corinthians 19
Genesis 1:24
Galatians 6:7
II Corinthians 13:5
John 1:3
Job 4:14
John 10:30
Ephesians 4:4-6
Genesis 1:11
Deuteronomy 32:18

About the Author

Neville Lancelot Goddard (1905–1972), was a New Thought pioneer, lecturer, and mystic who wrote on the Bible, esotericism and is considered to be a founder of the "law of assumption". Goddard was born in Barbados on February 19, 1905 to Joseph Nathaniel and Wilhelmina Goddard. He emigrated to New York City in the 1920s, where he first worked as a professional dancer.

In 1931, Neville began to study under an Ethiopian rabbi who introduced him to the Kabbalah. After a brief stint in the Army, he officially became a United States citizen. In the 1950s, Goddard lectured at The Town Hall on the many religious topics which served as the source of this book.

Neville's legacy includes greatly inspiring great minds like Rhonda Byrne and Wayne Dyer, as well as Carlos Castaneda.

ALSO BY ALIO PUBLISHING GROUP

THE MYSTERY OF CHRIST: The Bible Decoded
by Neville Goddard VOLUME TWO
(Autumn 2023)

Pay it Forward (and Back): A Gratitude Journal
and Daily Planner to Attract Abundance
(Available Now)

Meditation in 7 Pages
(Available Now)

Finding Your Voice: A Practical
Self Help Guide to Stop Stuttering
(Available Now)

Spirit Speaks Louder Than Words:
an unconventional memoir
(Available Now)

www.ingramcontent.com/pod-product-compliance
Lightning Source LLC
Chambersburg PA
CBHW060818050426
42449CB00008B/1709